All-Time Favorite
Parking Lot Picker's Mandoli

by Dix Bruce

40 mandolin solos of All-Time Favorite Bluegrass, Old-Time, and Gospel Songs!
• Songs, solos, & techniques every mandolin player should know!
• Melodies • Tablature • Chords • Solos recorded slow and up to speed
• Great for beginners and intermediates!

Online Audio   www.melbay.com/21369BCDEB

Audio Contents

© 2012 BY MEL BAY PUBLICATIONS, INC., PACIFIC, MO 63069.

Visit us on the Web at www.melbay.com   E-mail us at email@melbay.com.

Contents

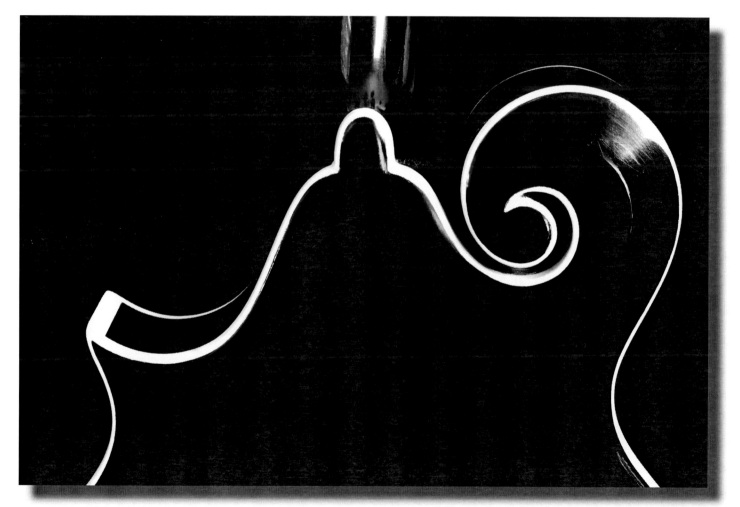

Detail from Kentucky KM-1000 early 1980s

Introduction

Welcome to the *All-Time Favorite Parking Lot Picker's Mandolin Solos* book/audio set! It's a collection of **40 mandolin solos** in a range of styles and levels of difficulty. You will find them useful if you are an advanced beginner to intermediate mandolinist who plays bluegrass, old-time, folk, or country music.

My main objective was to provide a wide range of solos on some of the most performed bluegrass, old-time, and gospel songs. These songs are played by musicians all over the world. You're likely to encounter them at jam sessions, picking parties, in bands, and on stage.

Almost all the solos are from songs initially published in my *Parking Lot Picker's Songbooks*. Now, mind you, not *every* song from *The Parking Lot Picker's Songbook* is included here because that songbook is quite comprehensive and contains over 215 songs. Instead I chose a representative sampling of what I believe to be some of the most important songs to know and to be able to solo on.

By the way, if you don't yet have a copy of *The Parking Lot Picker's Songbook* you should check it out. I know you'll enjoy it and, as they used to say on TV, "no home should be without one!" The solos in this book are for mandolin but *The Parking Lot Picker's Songbooks* are published in six separate editions, one each for mandolin, guitar, banjo, dobro, fiddle, and bass.

Variety of Solos

All-Time Favorite Parking Lot Picker's Mandolin Solos is filled with solos in a variety of bluegrass styles and subgenres. Though it's not meant to be a method book, we'll cover a lot of territory and address many technical issues unique to the mandolin. Here's a list of the types of solos we'll explore:

- Easy, open position single string solos
- closed position, moveable and transposable single string solos
- solos with tremolo
- open position double stop solos
- closed position double stop solos up the fingerboard
- solos with a distinct bluesy sound
- cross picking solos
- back up mandolin parts
- solos written in different regions of the mandolin fingerboard.

As you can see in the list above, I've also included a few pieces that aren't solos at all, they're parts a mandolinist would play while backing up a vocalist. Playing back up is a skill that every mandolinist should develop.

For several of the songs I included two solos of different types so that you can compare and contrast different approaches to the same song. Taken altogether the solos in this book present a good collection of many of the things every journeyman mandolinist should know how to do.

Why learn solos?

Solos give us the opportunity of playing our version of a melody. It's the instrumental version of telling a story. We want our solos to reflect our feelings and points of view as well as to show off our technique.

Solos can be a close representation of whatever melody we're working with or they can be an abstraction with little resemblance to the original. We'll work with several different approaches to taking a melody and turning it into a solo in this book.

In order to tell a story, we'll need to develop certain skills. As with speaking or writing, we'll need a vocabulary in order to play a good solo. We'll also need to build techniques that allow us to interpret ideas and tell the story. As a mandolin player we'll want to first learn a melody and then, with our various techniques, tell the tale.

A solo is like a short story and the notes and musical passages are our words, phrases, and expressions of ideas. As with speaking or writing, we won't just use a word or a phrase once, we'll learn it, tuck it away, and use it again and again to express similar or different ideas, in different passages, stories, etc. And, since so much of this repertoire follows familiar patterns of notes, tonalities, chord changes and so on, we can adapt a huge amount of what we learn on one song, whether it's melodic movement, licks, phrases, etc., to thousands of other songs.

As you learn the solos in this book you'll build your vocabulary of musical phrases, licks, positions, fingerings, picking styles, and all the rest. You can also use these solos as an opportunity to study how I took the idea of a basic melody, or the basic tune of a song, and turned it into a solo. You'll be able to use these building blocks in solos that you compose yourself for different songs. We'll discuss each solo with that goal in mind. Eventually you'll build on these solos and make them your own. Or, you'll strike out on your own with a given melody and create something entirely new and different.

Chord and Scale tones

Songs in this style, which we can generally refer to as bluegrass–old-time–folk–country, just like songs in other styles, follow certain conventions to make them fit into the style. I find that in bluegrass, country, old time, and folk music, melodies tend to favor chord tones. Chord tones are the first, third, and fifth tones of the chord's scale. For example, the chord tones for a G *major* chord are the notes G, B, and D, which are the first, third, and fifth tones of the G major scale. The same holds true for any major chord. Thus a C major chord is made up of the first, third, and fifth tones of the C major scale. Those notes are C, E, and G.

Chord recipes change somewhat depending on the type of chord your play. If you're playing a *minor* chord, let's say an Am, its chord tones will be the first, the *flatted third*, and the fifth of the A major scale. Those notes are A, C, and E. When we flat a note we lower it by one half step. In this case, the third tone of the A major scale is a C sharp (♯). If we flat the C♯ it becomes a C natural.

Seventh chords, also called *dominant seventh chords*, like A7, B7, E7, F7, B♭7 and so on, have yet another recipe. Dominant seventh chords are made up of the first, third, fifth, and *flatted seventh* tones of the associated major scale. A C7 chord would consist of the notes C, E, G, and B♭.

Generally speaking, of the chord tones in melodies, 1s (or roots) are probably used the most. Melodies often begin and end on 1s. 5s seem to be next in line followed by 3s. This, of course, is a very general observation on my part. Certain melodies avoid 1s altogether and center around the 5 or possibly the 3. It all depends on the specifics of the melody and those specifics define what a melody sounds like.

When melodies don't use chord tones they often use neighboring tones from the key's major scale. Here are two major scales diagrammed:

C	D	E	F	G	A	B	C
1	2	3	4	5	6	7	8
do	*re*	*me*	*fa*	*so*	*la*	*ti*	*do*

G	A	B	C	D	E	F♯	G
1	2	3	4	5	6	7	8
do	*re*	*me*	*fa*	*so*	*la*	*ti*	*do*

1 and 8 are both roots and the same note an *octave* (eight notes) apart.

Of the remaining notes 2s and 6s are probably next in popularity. 4s are more rare and 7s even more so. That doesn't mean you won't have melodies with all the notes of the scale or melodies that make copious use of 2s, 6s, 4s, or 7s. I'm just talking about tendencies. You might even have notes that are not chord or even scale tones. One example would be *blue notes* (flat 3s and flat 7s). If a melody includes notes not from the major scale, these notes tend to define that melody and set it apart. Try to evaluate how the melody is put together and, for the most part, if you're hunting for a note, look to the chord tones first, the 1s, 5s, 3s, then 2s, 6s, 4s, and 7s, then the blue notes. I tend to search in that order of prominence. Because the melodic formulas are so similar from song to song it's important that you learn the scales in different keys and also familiarize yourself with the chord tones. Luckily learning the scales in different keys is fairly easy on the mandolin.

Is it OK to compose a solo and then always perform it?

It's better than not having a solo at all or playing something that doesn't sound good! I compose solos and perform them again and again, though not necessarily exactly the same each time. I find that gradually, by repetition, a composed solo starts to change all on its own. If I start to get tired of the same old solo, I'll also try to change it a bit and eventually I'll try to compose a 2nd, 3rd, or 4th solo. Once I have these mastered, I find that I start swapping parts in and out of different solos and re-combine them into totally new solos. It's an exciting process that, over time, builds your repertoire of licks, themes, riffs, solos and vocabulary. It's a win-win situation. You do have to start somewhere and master that first solo and I hope that the solos in this book will provide you with some starting points. You don't have to learn the solos exactly as I present them. Feel free to change them whenever you feel like it. The important thing though, is to get something down, something memorized, something definite and focused, that you can play when the need arises. For me that means that I have to memorize a phrase or solo and practice it until I can play it in all kinds of situations.

Level of Difficulty

The solos aren't presented in any particular order though most of the easier ones are grouped more toward the beginning of the book. Depending on your level of accomplishment on the mandolin you may find some things very easy and other things difficult. Keep in mind that everyone will have strengths and weaknesses and techniques that are new to you may take a little while to get used to and master. Just about everybody has "issues" with double stop tremolo, cross picking, and playing in closed positions when they first explore those techniques. Hang in there, with practice it'll get easier! I hope you will try to play all of the solos.

Additional Solos

As I mentioned above, a few of the songs are presented with more than one solo. I thought it would be interesting and educational to explore different solo ideas for the same melody. Why would you need more than one solo for any given song? You might be participating in a small jam session where, during a performance of one song, you get more than one turn to solo. Of course, you could certainly play your one solo two, three, or four times, but it might be more interesting to play something different each time around. One of the nice things about learning multiple solos to the same song is that you can cherry pick musical phrases and licks from the various solos to create even more solos. Remember: in learning all these different solos you're building a system of compiling musical vocabulary, phrases, and syntax. Anything you learn can be applied to multiple musical situations and songs.

The recordings

All the solos are recorded on the play–along audio at two speeds: slow and regular. The main point of the audio is to show you how the solo sounds but you'll learn a lot faster if you try playing along with the recordings first at the slow speed and later, when you're ready, at the regular speed.

Track 1 of the audio has tones to tune to. (I loved writing that!) Track locations for the slow and regular speed recordings are shown on page 1 and on each solo to the left of the title. The recordings are mixed (mandolin in the right channel, guitar in the left channel) so that you can isolate both the lead mandolin part and the guitar accompa-niment. Adjust the balance control on your stereo to hear more or less of one or the other part. If you are listening on headphones and don't have a dedicated balance control you can take one ear piece or the other off partially or completely to simulate the same balance control.

I kept the regular speed versions of the solos at a pretty moderate tempo. In the real world, you can play them at whatever speed you can muster and master. Just keep in mind that speed is only one aspect of playing well. Go for a clean and clear sound and don't worry so much about speed. Most of us would rather hear something slow and clean than fast and sloppy. Am I right?

You may find it difficult to make the transition from the slow speed version of a solo to the regular speed version. If that's the case you might want to check out software that can speed up or slow down audio files independent of changing the pitch. I've had great luck with a program called "The Amazing Slow Downer" though I know there are several similar programs available. It's available for computers, smart phones, and iPads. The computer version, which is what I have used, cost about $50 and it's been worth every cent. As of this writing the full-featured "The Amazing Slow Downer" is downloadable to mobile devices for about $15. With this type of software you can slow down or speed up audio files in very small increments. It's a great way to progress gradually.

I also find metronomes to be very helpful in getting a solo up to speed. At any point in developing the solo all you need to do is practice with the metronome set at a comfortable speed. Next decide what your up-to-speed goal is and work toward it in increments of three to five clicks on the metronome. You can use a metronome in exactly the same way you'd use a slow downer. I suggest that you keep track of your work and progress in a bound music notebook. That way you'll have all your work and notes together in one place. I find that notebooks are somewhat more difficult to lose or misplace than a single sheet of paper.

These days you'll find you have numerous metronome choices. You can still find the old-fashioned mechanical models but electronic, battery-operated models are much more economical and available. Of course if you're really on the cutting edge you can use a metronome that's available on the Internet or download one for your smart phone or iPad. Several are available free of charge.

Working with the solos

When you first start working on a solo, it's a good idea to slowly play through the music while you listen to the recordings. Work through the solo slowly and figure out all the finger moves before you try to play along. Once you feel fairly comfortable on your own try playing along with the slow version of the solo. Work with the slow version of the solo until you have it mastered. Only then should you begin working with the regular speed version. As I mentioned above, if you have trouble making the leap from the slow to the regular speed version, approach it gradually either with the help of a metronome or by using the type of software we discussed.

Some of the solos are written with repeats and first and second endings. I'll discuss them as they appear in the book but keep in mind that you don't have to play the parts exactly the same on the repeat. In fact when I'm performing I almost automatically make some little change here or there just to make things a little bit more interesting for me and the audience. That said, there's nothing wrong with playing the exact same part both times. The traditional style of bluegrass soloing is to keep the variation to a minimum and play good melodies that the audience can understand and relate to the song at hand. Of course, if you have an audience that's paying attention, throwing in some unexpected notes and runs here and there can be exciting and they'll love you for it. If the audience is less than attentive, changing things up can at the very least, amuse you and your fellow musicians.

There's no right or wrong as to what to change or to what degree to change it. For guidance listen to your favorite instrumentalists, not just mandolin players but any instrumentalists, and see how they do it. For example, I learned a lot from the late, great Earl Scruggs. His playing is so simple that it's difficult! On any number of recordings you can hear him play basically the same solo again and again but change only a note or two each time. He sets up a theme on an earlier solo that the audience can remember and then kind of comments on it in his later solos. It's a wonderful approach. The incomparable Maybelle Carter of the Carter Family played in much the same way.

Fretting finger numbers are shown between the standard music notation staff and the tablature staff. These reflect the fretting fingers that I use. Try them. If you find you can't reach some of these fingerings change them.

Fretting finger moves like hammer ons (*h*), slides (*s*), and pull offs (*p*), are noted under the standard music notation.

Measure numbers are shown above the treble clef sign beginning in staff two of every solo. These numbers are counted from the first full measure and do not include any pickup measures.

Additional downloadable solos
On many of the solos I'll suggest additional exercises like moving a solo to another key or another area of the fingerboard. I hope you'll try all of these additional projects as they'll deepen your understanding of the mandolin. I've posted several of these solos or exercises on my website: **http://www.musixnow.com/plpmandosolos. html**. All you have to do is log on and grab 'em.

Keys
A lot of the bluegrass, old-time, gospel, folk, and country repertoire tends to be played in the keys of G and C. I'm not quite sure why that is. It may have something to do with the relative ease of playing in these keys, especially for guitar players. It may also have to do with typical singers' ranges. As I was putting together *The Parking Lot Picker's Songbooks* I noticed that these keys are quite prevalent in the recordings made by the classic performers and inventors of the style. Of course, you'll find a variety of other keys in evidence too: D, A, E, B♭, B, among others.

There are several determining factors in choosing a key. For example, fiddlers like the keys of D and A. Singers like whatever key is best for their voice and that key might not be G or C, but instead might be B or B♭. Guitar and banjo players can play in most keys with ease by using a capo. They simply hold the chords of the key of G, C, etc., and by placing the capo at different frets on the fingerboard change the sound of that key to many different keys.

As a mandolinist you need to be prepared to play in any key. Though we don't generally use mandolin capos, the good news is that it's relatively easy to move things around on the mandolin. That's because the mandolin is tuned in fifths. Each string, beginning with the thinnest or first string, E (1) – A (2) – D (3) – G (4), is tuned a musical interval of a *fifth* away from its neighbor. That's not the case on the guitar where four of the intervals between strings are *fourths* and the other interval is a *third* (between strings two and three). This standard guitar tuning makes it very difficult to move things around. We are lucky to be mandolin players! And, never forget this: as a mandolin player the world is your oyster!

Open or closed position?
In the listing of solo types above I mentioned the terms "open" and "closed" position. Solos are identified as "open" if they include unfretted or open string notes. Solos are identified as "closed" if all their notes are fretted and include no open string notes. It's typical for beginning players to play simple leads in open positions with open string notes. As you advance you'll want to learn to play the same solos in closed positions. Each position has unique tonal qualities and as such is worth exploring and mastering. The great advantage of playing passages or solos in closed positions is that they can be moved to just about any key with ease. It's much more difficult to move around a passage or solo that includes open string notes. With that in mind I placed many of the solos in this book

in closed, and thus moveable, positions. Closed position solos are no more difficult to learn than open position solos and, once you have learned and memorized them, you'll be able to play them in any key!

Why is that important? Because chances are very good that as soon as you start playing with other people they'll know the same songs you know in different keys. They may have learned a song in a key like B$^\flat$ to accommodate their vocal range. Since the singer can't change his or her vocal range — it is what it is — you, as a mandolinist, need to be able to play in their key. This book will give you practice in many different keys and help you toward the goal of playing comfortably in any key.

Musix website: http://www.musixnow.com

I hope you'll visit my Musix website. The link is above. There you'll find complete information on all my books, CDs, and videos plus sample pages, audio, and video from most of my projects. I especially hope you'll check out the *Musix Newsletter* section of the site. There you'll find tons of downloadable lessons, music, TAB, and audio files, all for free.

Well, that's probably enough verbiage from me for a while. I bet you're itching to get to the solos. Dive right in and have some fun!

Dix Bruce, Fall 2012

Photo by K. Bruce Photography

About the author:

Dix Bruce is a musician and writer from the San Francisco Bay Area. He has authored over fifty books, recordings, and videos for Mel Bay Publications. Dix performs and does studio work on mandolin, guitar, bass, and banjo. He has recorded two LPs with mandolin legend Frank Wakefield, eight big band CDs with the Royal Society Jazz Orchestra, his own collection of American folk songs entitled *My Folk Heart* on which he plays guitar, mandolin, autoharp and sings; and a CD of string swing and jazz entitled *Tuxedo Blues*. He has released four CDs of traditional American songs and originals with guitarist Jim Nunally, most recently a collection of brother duet style recordings entitled *Brothers at Heart*. Dix arranged, composed, and played mandolin on the soundtracks to four different editions of the best selling computer game *The Sims*. For a complete listing of Dix s publications, log onto his website: http://www.musixnow.com.

Also by Dix Bruce:

Getting into Bluegrass Mandolin, book/CD set
First Lessons: Mandolin, book/CD set
Gypsy Swing & Hot Club Rhythm for Mandolin, Vol. I & II, two different book/CD sets
You Can Teach Yourself Mandolin, book/CD set
Favorite Mandolin Picking Tunes, book/CD set
Mandolin Uff Da! Let's Dance: Scandinavian Fiddle Tunes & House Party Music, book/CD set
Dix Bruce's Swing & Jazz Mandolin: Chords, Rhythm, and Songs, DVD
BackUP Trax: Old Time & Fiddle Tunes, book/CD set
Christmas Crosspicking Solos for Guitar, book/CD set
Christmas Favorites for Solo Guitar (30 Best Loved Traditional Songs for Bluegrass Guitar), book/CD set
The Parking Lot Picker's Songbooks, six different book/2CD sets

Join Dix online at http://www.musixnow.com & download free Musix Newsletters, music, TAB, & MP3s.

BRW LP H3 mandolin, 2012

Bury Me Beneath the Willow

Arrangement © 2012 by Dix Bruce

"Bury Me Beneath the Willow" is a good example of taking a simple melody and turning it into a solo by adding up and down picked eighth notes. This sound is reminiscent of the early bluegrass, early Bill Monroe style. That mandolin style is abundantly evident in the recordings of the Monroe Brothers, Charlie and Bill, from the mid-1930s. I recommend a great four-CD set from JSP records entitled *Bill Monroe and his Bluegrass Boys 1937-1949*. The first two of four CDs has the complete Monroe Brothers recorded output. The other two CDs are Monroe's first recordings with a five-piece bluegrass band. Not only will you hear this exciting style of mandolin soloing, you'll hear many of the classic songs that comprise the traditional bluegrass repertoire, including this very song "Bury Me Beneath the Willow." If you haven't yet heard this music you'll be amazed by its passion, precision, and speed.

The near continuous "down-up" picking that you'll see throughout this solo is quite typical of bluegrass mandolin. For pick directions I usually use a down pick for notes that fall on beats 1, 2, 3, 4 (or beats 1, 2, 3 if the song is a waltz) and up picks on the "ands" between the numbered beats. Here's a diagram:

1	and	2	and	3	and	4	and
↓	↑	↓	↑	↓	↑	↓	↑

There are slides, shown between the staffs with a small italic "*s*," in measures 4, 7, 9, 12. With slides you'll fret and pick the note about two frets below where you want to end up. To play the slide in measure 4, fret the fourth string at about the second fret, pick the note and immediately slide up the fret four on the same string. I say "about" because you can slide up to a note from 1 or 2 frets below. It's up to you. You can also slide into a note from an open string. ***Key of D.***

Schneider #49 by Bob Schneider, 2005

Bury Me Beneath the Willow

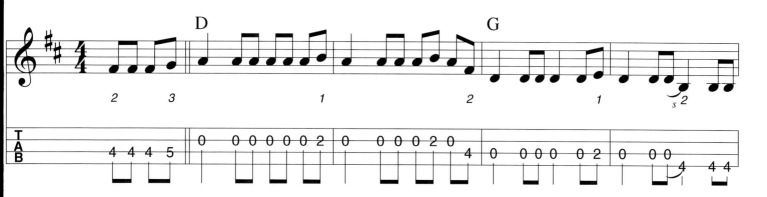

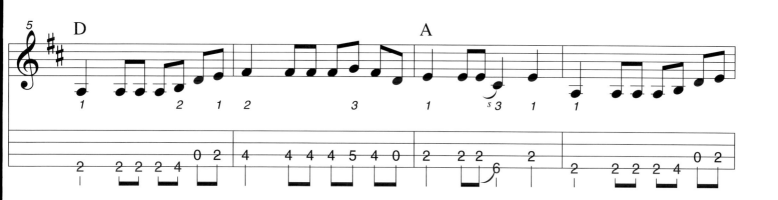

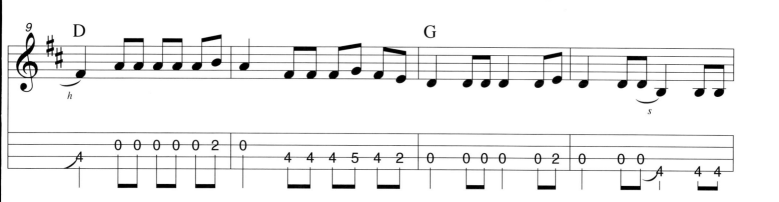

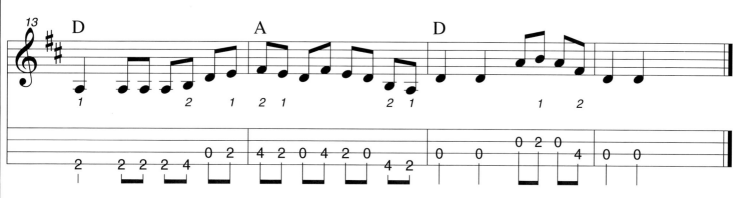

All -Time Favorite Parking Lot Picker's Mandolin Solos by Dix Bruce 13

Long Journey Home

Arrangement © 2012 by Dix Bruce

"Long Journey Home" is another Monroe-esque solo with near constant down-up eighth note patterns. The song is also a bluegrass classic recorded by the Monroe Brothers in the 1930s. I use down strokes on all the notes that fall on beats one, two, three, and four, and up strokes on the notes that fall on the "ands" between the numbered beats. See the pick direction diagram in page 12. Be sure to master this type of picking at the slow speed before you try to speed it up. Bill Monroe played this at a breakneck speed, which was easy for him. Give it some practice and time and you'll get up to that speed as well. ***Key of G.***

Shady Grove

"Shady Grove" is a beautiful song that I first heard played by the late, great Doc Watson. These days audiences are familiar with "Shady Grove" from the recording of the same name by Jerry Garcia and David Grisman. This version would be considered more old time than bluegrass.

"Shady Grove" is written here as a double solo. Depending on how you perform it you might use one or both. The first solo, measures 1 through 8, is relatively easier than the second with its mixed quarter and eight notes and fretted and open string notes. The second solo, measures 9 through 16, will take you into the upper reaches of the fingerboard. If you're not used to playing up there, it can be a challenge, especially for the pinkie on your fretting hand. But I can assure you that any effort you expend up in these regions will pay off handsomely. The more you do it the easier it will become. As you practice you'll start to see the relationships between notes in a key and patterns will start to emerge that you'll use again and again on other similar songs. Be sure to stick with it. If the second solo is just too difficult for you right now and you need a 16 measure solo, play the first solo twice through.

I've listed this song as being pitched in the key of E minor (Em) but that's not quite the whole story. It would be more musically correct to say that this solo is in E minor modal. The key signature of "Shady Grove" has two sharps in it and those two sharps, F♯ and C♯, define the key of D major. But, as you listen to "Shady Grove," you'll hear that it doesn't sound like it's in a major key. It's kind of in between a major and a minor tonality and that sound is often identified as "modal." There are several different types of modes. This particular mode could also be described as "dorian." That's because it's built on the second tone of the D major scale. That note is an E. If all this music theory confounds and frustrates you just ignore it and enjoy playing "Shady Grove"! ***Key of Em.***

Weber Bitterroot A, 2007 (l.) and Pomeroy PA 4, 2008 (r.) A-style mandolins.

Shady Grove

Arrangement © 2012 by Dix Bruce

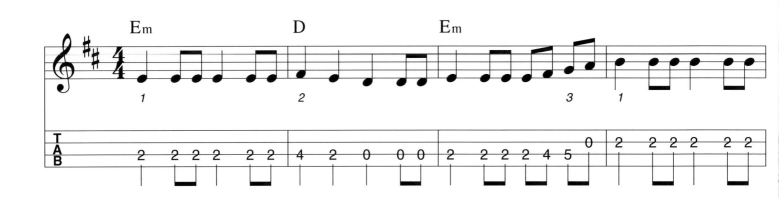

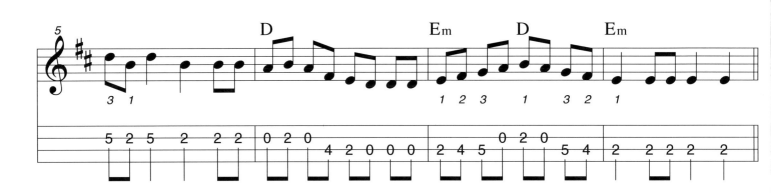

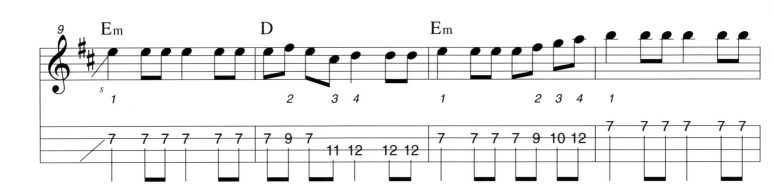

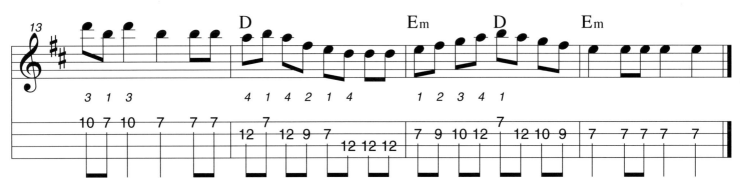

Tracks 8 & 9

Wabash Cannonball

Arrangement © 2012 by Dix Bruce

I included "Wabash Cannonball" because it's such a popular old song seemingly played by every bluegrass, folk, and country musician everywhere. That may be a slight overstatement but it's certainly a "must know" song.

The melody to "Wabash Cannonball" is quite simple and made up mostly of quarter notes. I wanted the solo to be a bit more interesting, so for the most part, I turned those quarter notes into eighth notes which you'll play with a fairly continuous "down–up" picking pattern. For extra texture there are some quarter notes mixed in along with the slides in measures 5 and 13. *Key of G.*

Tracks 10 & 11

Amazing Grace

Arrangement © 2012 by Dix Bruce

"Amazing Grace" is a basic single string solo with mixed fretted and open string notes. I suggest that you tremolo notes longer than quarters. If you find that too difficult just play the notes without tremolo. In the long run though, the tremolo is a large part of the sound of this style of mandolin and you'll want to include it when you perform the solo.

Let's talk a bit about transposing solos and passages that include open string notes. This solo would be difficult to automatically transpose to the key of, say, A♭ or F. **However, since the mandolin is so superior to all the other instruments, we can still do some limited, virtually automatic transposing.** Look at the tablature. Notice that all the notes are played on the middle two strings: strings 2, the A string, and 3, the D. Once you've memorized the solo as written try starting it on string number 2, instead of string number 3. If you play the notes in the same fret locations but on these new strings you'll move the solo up to the key of D. Pretty easy, huh? Now let's go back to our original solo and this time, try starting it on string number 4, the G string. Play all the other notes in the same frets as before but on the new strings. By moving the solo in this way you'll transpose it from the key of G to the key of C. If you have difficulty visualizing or executing these moves you can download the music and tab for both solos from my website. Here's the address: http://www.musixnow.com/plpmandosolos.html. ***Key of G.***

Nine Pound Hammer

Arrangement © 2012 by Dix Bruce

"Nine Pound Hammer" is another solo written in the early bluegrass, Monroe-esque style. It's a bit more challenging than a solo like "Bury Me Beneath the Willow" or "Long Journey Home" as I've added lots of neighboring eighth note tones to the general flow of melody. Be sure to listen to how Bill Monroe plays this song, particularly on his recordings with the Monroe Brothers. Don't expect to play at his breakneck speed today or tomorrow. Give yourself at least a couple weeks! ***Key of A.***

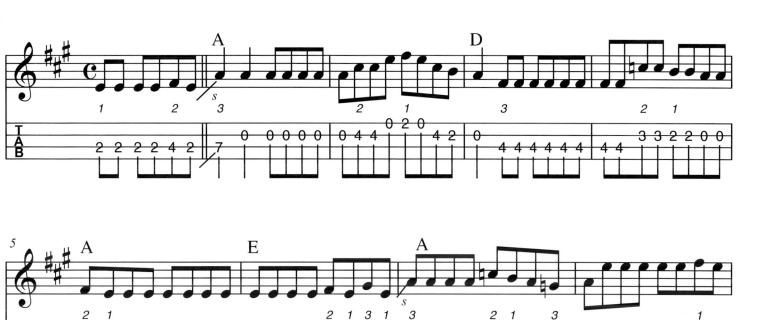

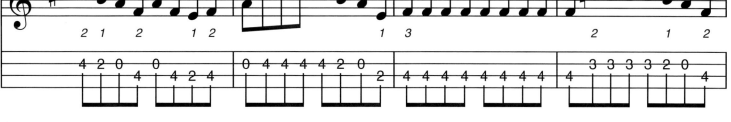

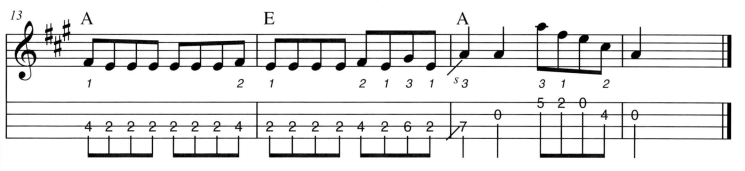

Banks of the Ohio *basic solo*

Here's a pretty solo on the classic song "Banks of the Ohio." The solo is a mixture of single note and double stop tremolo playing. Most of the double stops have at least one open string note. Because of that, this solo is a little difficult to move up and down the fingerboard to a variety of keys. However, you can move it over a string to a new key. You'll find a more advanced, crosspicking solo to "Banks of the Ohio" on page 46.

If a solo is played on one string on the mandolin we can move it over to three other strings and play the same solo in three additional keys. If a solo is played on two strings we can move it over to two other sets of two strings and play the same solo in two additional keys. This "Banks of the Ohio" solo is played on three strings: the second, the third, and the fourth. We can move this solo over to one other set of three strings. If we start the solo on the third string, second fret instead of the fourth string, second fret and essentially move the note positions over one string each we'll transpose it from the key of D, as written, to the key of A.

It's important to keep in mind that while solos with open strings might not be as readily movable up and down the fingerboard as solos with all fretted notes, they do have a unique timbre. They sound different from solos with all fretted notes. As such, open string solos and passages offer different tonal colors and are worth knowing for that reason alone.

You'll play a lot of long, legato, double stop tremolo notes in this solo. Look for the whole notes tied over the measure line to either quarter notes or half notes. You'll need to keep your tremolo going for a long time. Try to get it to sound like a kind of relaxed buzz. In order to do that you have to keep your picking hand quite loose and limber. If it's tight the tremolo won't sound right and your hand will get fatigued before you've finished playing the extended note. David Grisman has just about the most beautiful and expressive tremolo in the world. Listen to what he does with tremolo and try to make those same sounds yourself. ***Key of D.***

Gibson A-model, early 1920s

Tracks 14 & 15

Banks of the Ohio

Arrangement © 2012 by Dix Bruce

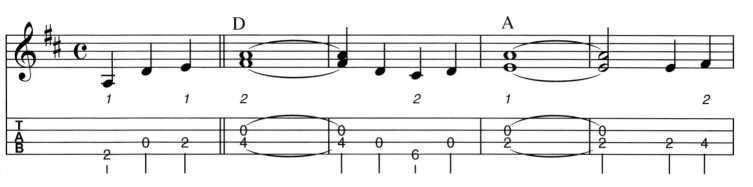

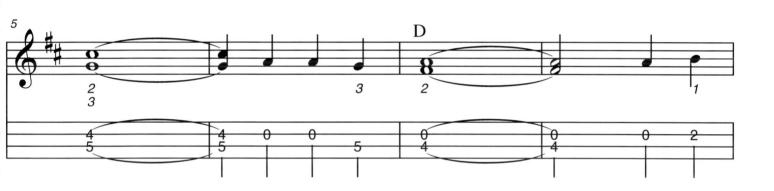

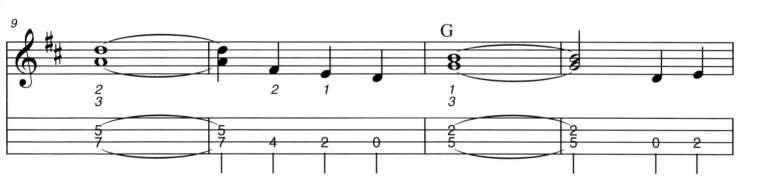

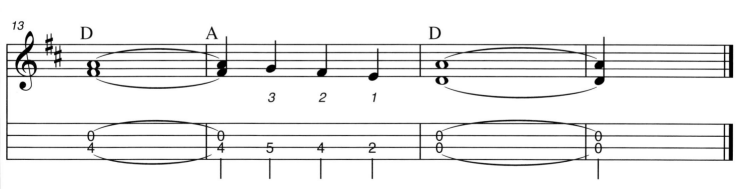

All the Good Times are Past and Gone *back up part*

Let's leave the solos behind briefly and spend a little time looking at a back up part. Later in the book, on page 40, you'll learn a solo for "All the Good Times." Back up parts are usually played behind singing. Your sacred duty is to support the singer and make him or her sound his or her best. Take care to not play too loud or play anything that distracts the audience's attention from the main event: the singing. If the audience is more aware of your playing than what the singer is singing, you have failed. Don't compete with the singer. Try to complement what he or she is doing and build an ensemble sound. It's a delicate thing to master but when you do master it, singers and audiences alike will love you for it. For demonstration purposes the mandolin is mixed quite a bit louder on the recording than it would be in an actual band situation backing up a vocal. Also, I played a mandolin lead on the slow version since it was a little too slow to sing to.

This particular back up part for "All the Good Times" is made up of double stops played with tremolo. In case you're not familiar with the term "double stop" it's when we play two notes on two different strings at the same time. Tremolo is where we play rapid up and down strokes to make a long, legato, sound on the mandolin. Tremolo allows mandolinists to extend a note indefinitely, like a violinist's bow.

The arrangement shown gives you three separate but similar back up parts. You'll find subtle differences between them. If you're not used to either the double stop or the tremolo technique this "All the Good Times" back up part may be a challenge to you at first. Play the parts slowly and don't speed them up until you're comfortable with the techniques.

All three parts are written with repeats and first and second endings. As I mentioned in the introduction to this book, feel free to change your playing on the repeats if you feel so inspired. Of course, you don't have to change a thing but if the spirit moves you, have at it!

All three parts are written in closed positions. That makes them easy to transpose to different keys. Try moving the parts up two frets to the key of A. Once you can do that, move them up another fret to the key of B♭ and so on.

Try moving Back up #1 across the fingerboard. Play the first notes on strings 1 and 2 instead of strings 2 and 3. Keep the fret numbers the same. If you do it correctly you'll transpose the part up in pitch to the key of D. Now go back to the original version of Back up #1 and move it in the other direction across the fingerboard. Play the first notes on strings 3 and 4 instead of strings 2 and 3 and keep the fret numbers the same. This will move the part down in pitch to the key of C. Ain't that just too cool?

You can do just about the same thing with Back up #2 and 3 but since they span three strings instead of two, you can only move them up in pitch to the key of D. Be sure to experiment with these types of transposing on *all* the solos and parts in this book. It can be difficult at first, but the more you do it, the easier it will become. ***Key of G.***

All the Good Times are Past and Gone *back up parts*

Arrangement © 2012 by Dix Bruce

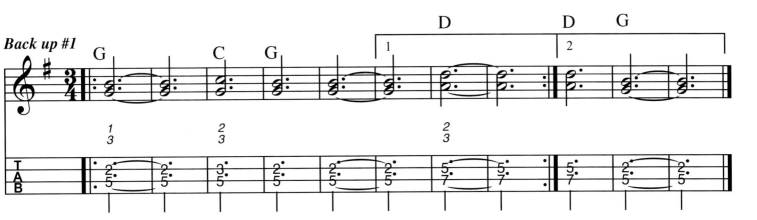

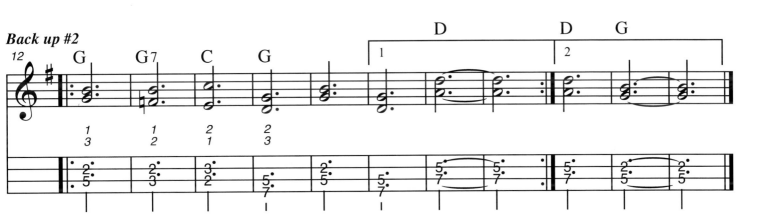

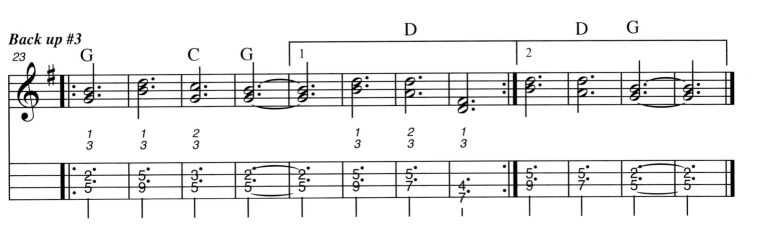

Angel Band *back up part*

While we're in the back up mode, here's another back up part to play behind the vocal on a great and be-loved song, "Angel Band." It's made up, mostly, of long double stop tremolo notes with some ending licks added in. You'll notice that, except for the ending licks, the part is not melodic. That's because I wanted it to be a wash of notes behind the vocal that wouldn't compete with it.

As you may know, each chord suggests several double stop positions with different notes in each. You can see this in the first two measures under the G chord. The first double stop is played with the G note the lower of the pair and the B the higher. In the next measure we move up the fingerboard and the lower note of the double stop is a B, the upper note a D. I included quite a few of these alternate double stop pairs in the "Angel Band" back up so you could explore some of the many choices you have and where they reside on the fingerboard.

Though this part is written with repeats and first and second endings, just like I've mentioned before, there's no reason for you not to change the part slightly on the repeat.

Can you move this part around the fingerboard to different keys as you did with the "All the Good Times" back up part?

You'll find a double stop solo to "Angel Band" on page 43. ***Key of G.***

Headstock detail, Schneider #49 by Bob Schneider, 2005

Angel Band *back up part*

Arrangement © 2012 by Dix Bruce

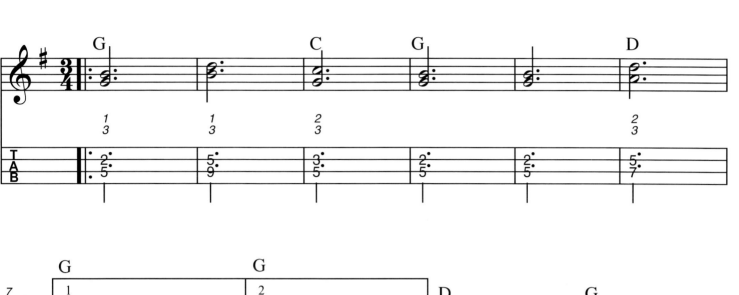

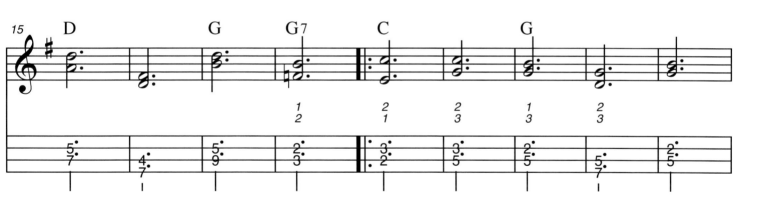

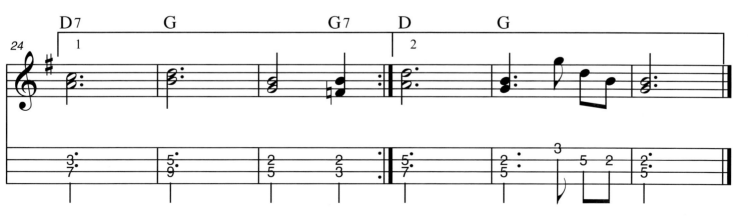

Don't Let Your Deal Go Down

"Don't Let Your Deal Go Down" is another important song that everyone plays and you should know how to play it too. It has a slightly unusual chord progression, more from the ragtime or pop world than from bluegrass or folk. "Don't Let Your Deal Go Down" is written in the key of G but the first chord is an E7. The chord progression continues with A7, D7, and then G. This type of progression is usually referred to as a "cycle of fifths progression." Dominant seventh chords like E7, A7, D7, G7, C7, etc. are also referred to as "fifths" or "five chords," hence the term "cycle of fifths progression."

The first eight measures of the solo are not particularly melodic. I saved that for the second eight measures. You can flip them if you'd like. Once again, fretting finger suggestions are important to follow especially in areas, like measures 1 and 2, where there are position shifts.

This solo works well on "Don't Let Your Deal Go Down" but you can also repurpose a lot of these musical passages to work over the same dominant chords in other songs. You may notice that for the most part the notes in the solo are closed position, fretted notes. That means that you can move them around, up and down and across the fingerboard. Practice moving measures one and two up three frets so that your first note is on the third string, fifth fret. The resulting lick will be a G7 lick. Now try moving this same E7 lick down in pitch by one string so your first note will be on the fourth string, second fret. By doing that you'll turn this into an A7 lick. Just about all of the passages will work the same way and if you put in a little work you can recycle them not only to different songs with the same chords but also transpose them to new chords. In the process you'll build your vocabulary and have a variety of passages to play over dominant seventh chords. Try to adapt these passages to the similar song "Salty Dog Blues."

The solo will take you to some new regions of the fingerboard where you'll employ some different fingerings then we've used previously. You'll use your fourth fretting finger quite a bit. You'll need that pinkie as you progress and grow as a mandolinist. Might as well start using it now! In that sense this solo is a little more difficult and a little more advanced than we've had. Still, it's not all that difficult. Give it a fair shake.

I added a few "bluesy" sounding notes to the solo: the F natural in measures 4, 7, and 8, and the Bb in measure 7. The blues play a major part in the bluegrass sound and you'll want to know where the blue notes lie on the mandolin so you can include them and spice up your solos. More on that later in the book. ***Key of G.***

Don't Let Your Deal Go Down

Arrangement © 2012 by Dix Bruce

Little Birdie *closed single string solo*

Here are two solos on one of my favorite traditional songs, "Little Birdie." The first "Little Birdie" solo is made up of mostly continuous down–up 1/8 notes. The second solo, on page 30, includes some double stops. The first is written in a closed position, all the notes are fretted, and it uses a closed G major scale position. The root or first note of the scale is played on the third string, fifth fret, with the first finger. Here's what that scale looks like:

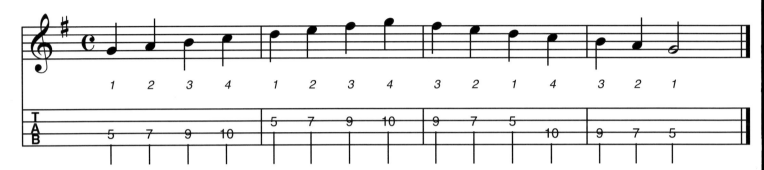

Since most of the songs in the bluegrass-old-time-country-folk repertoire are vocals, the range of notes they use are generally limited to a single octave plus a note or two above and below that octave. This scale shows some of the most likely notes above and below the scale. Obviously there are a few more, especially below the third string, fifth fret root. What are they? Fretting finger numbers are between the music and tablature staffs in *italic* type and scale note numbers are above the music staff in **bold** type.

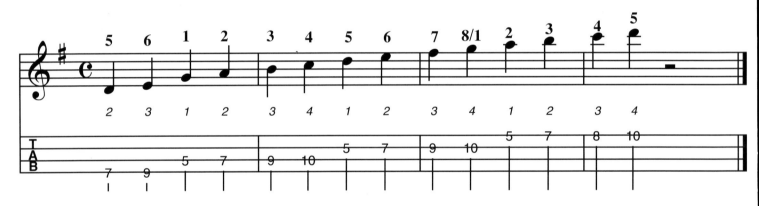

It makes sense then that if you learn where the scales are located you should be able to find the notes to just about any melody. By moving the scale position around to different root notes you'll be able to play a melody in any key. That's an awesome skill to develop.

This particular G major scale can be identified by which finger you use to play the root of the scale, in this case the first finger. Each different root/finger combination defines a different position where the major scale is played. You should also explore major scales where the root is played by the second, third, and fourth fingers. Once you can play a G major scale starting with the first finger, be sure to move that scale up, down, and across the fingerboard to as many different keys as you can find. Don't expect to master this in a week or a few months. Plan on spending a lot of time and eventually the knowledge and skill will kick in. ***Key of G.***

Little Birdie

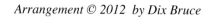
Arrangement © 2012 by Dix Bruce

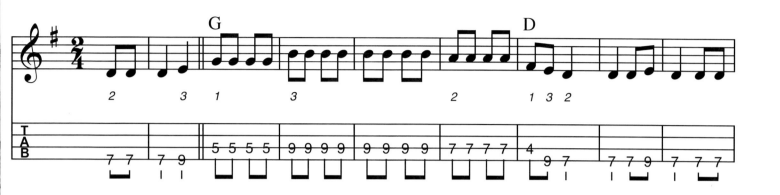

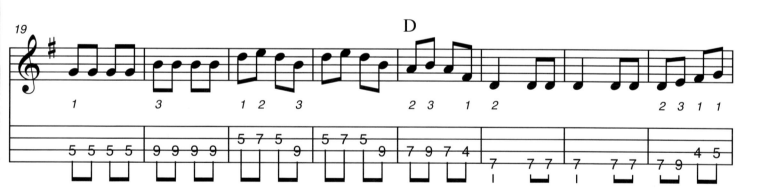

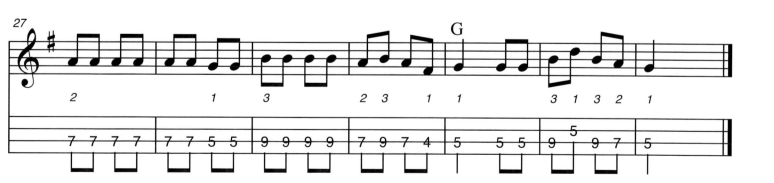

Little Birdie *double stop solo*

This double stop solo for "Little Birdie" uses the same general position and closed G major scale as the previous "Little Birdie" single string solo (page 28). This time, however, I've added quite a few double stops. Pay close attention to your fretting finger numbers.

As we've discussed earlier ("Banks of the Ohio" page 20), a double stop is simply two notes played at the same time on the mandolin. These notes can both be fretted, one fretted and one open, or both open string notes. In this style of music a lot of the double stops played are based around intervals of thirds. Of course if you play double stops throughout a melody you'll have a range of intervals between the two notes. Some of them can be quite a stretch for your fretting fingers.

I wanted to call attention to one type of double stop in this "Little Birdie" solo. I call it the "lazy" double stop. You'll see the first example of one in the first full measure where you'll play the third string G and the second string D both at the fifth fret with your first finger. You may have a little difficulty at first fretting two strings with one finger but if you give it some time it will improve and you'll find it quite useful.

This particular "lazy" double stop, two adjacent notes played with one finger, gives us the interval of a *perfect fifth*. You may be more used to the sound of a *major third*, which you'll find in the alternate measures at the bottom of the page. For this double stop you play a G note on the third string, fifth fret, with your third finger and at the same time play a B note on the second string, second fret, with your first finger. You can substitute in this double stop, G on the bottom, B on the top, anytime you see the "lazy" double stop with G on the bottom and D on the top.

The solo isn't made up of continuous double stops. In some measures, like measure 7, 16, and elsewhere, you'll be playing single string eighth notes. Including them adds some nice variations in the solo but you may find it difficult at first to make the transitions out of playing double stops and into playing single strings and back. Slow everything down and practice the transitions until they're smooth. ***Key of G.***

Headstock detail F5 Deluxe Nugget mandolin, 2005

Tracks 24 & 25

Little Birdie *double stop solo*

Arrangement © 2012 by Dix Bruce

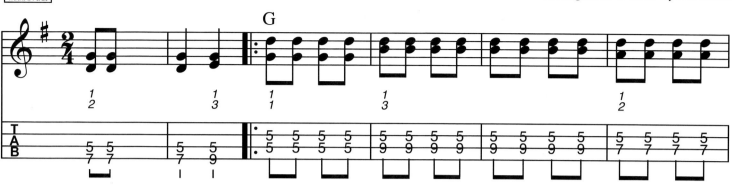

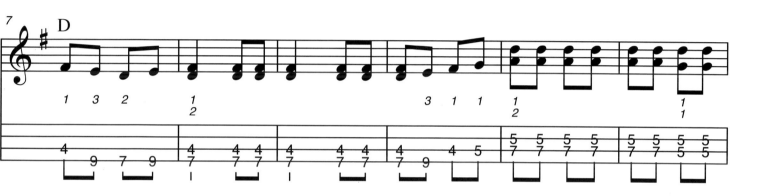

G   See alt. measures below

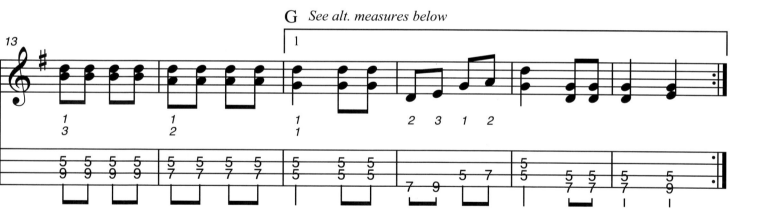

G   Alt. measures

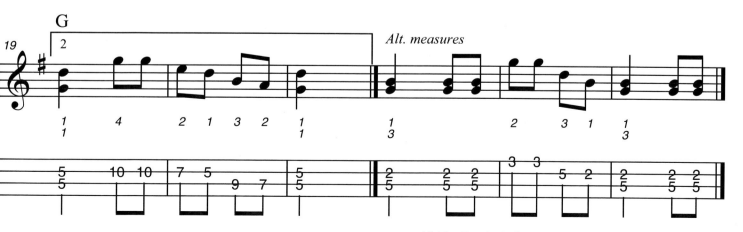

Down in the Valley to Pray

Arrangement © 2012 by Dix Bruce

You may be familiar with this song, and a whole list of other great ones, from its inclusion in the popular George Clooney movie "O Brother, Where Art Thou?" In the movie it was called "Down to the River to Pray." If you don't already have the movie soundtrack I think you'll enjoy it and the "Down from the Mountain (Live)" discs.

This very bluegrassy solo explores more of the upper closed position G scale. If you're not used to playing in this neighborhood of the fingerboard the suggested fretting finger numbers will help you find your way through the wilderness. As you can see from the music, the solo is made up of almost continual 1/8 notes in that early Monroe tradition. Watch for a tricky fretting finger move in measure 5 where your first finger will have to transition from the fourth string, fourth fret to the third string, fifth fret. Practice it slowly until it's smooth. Can you move this solo to different keys up and down the fingerboard? How about to different keys across the fingerboard? **Key of G.**

Feast Here Tonight

Arrangement © 2012 by Dix Bruce

"Feast Here Tonight" is also known as "Rabbit in the Log" because a rabbit in a log is the subject of the story told in the song. The solo has a traditional bluegrass, Monroe-esque feel to it due to the continual "down-up" eighth notes. "Feast Here Tonight" is another great song recorded by the Monroe Brothers. Again, don't feel like you have to play the solo at their speed. Work your way up gradually and concentrate on playing the notes cleanly and precisely. The solo is on the verse only. Listen to the Monroe Brothers and make up your own solo on the chorus.

In measure 14 and 15 I added in a few B♭ or "blue" notes. The B♭ notes are not part of the G major scale. To get them we're flatting the third or B note of the G major scale. So called "blue" notes are usually the flatted third and seventh notes from the major scale. The flatted seventh note would be an F natural. They give the solo a bit of a blues flavor, just like Bill did on so many of his classic recordings. ***Key of G.***

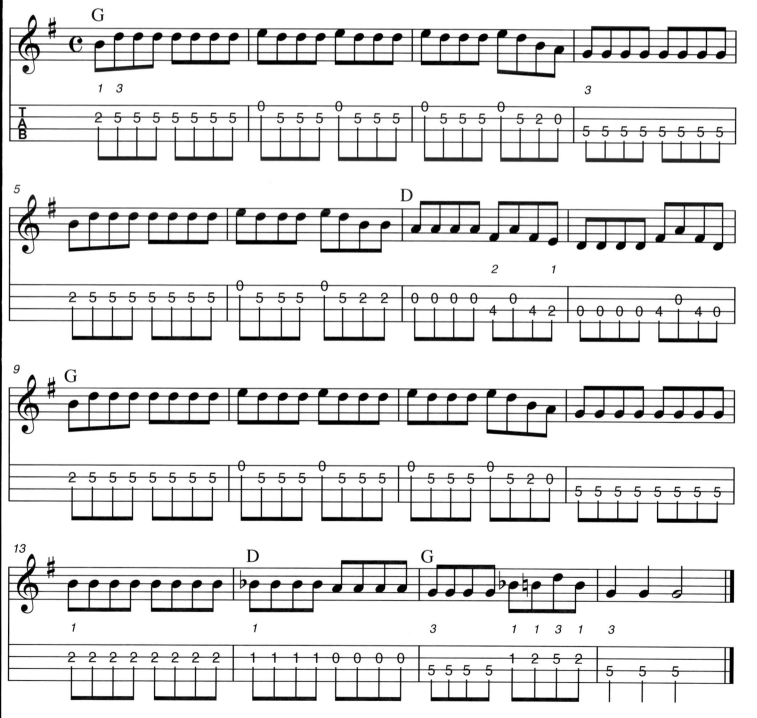

Cripple Creek

Arrangement © 2012 by Dix Bruce

      "Cripple Creek" is another one of those songs that you need to know. It turns up again and again at jam sessions. This version includes two separate solos. The first is made up mostly of quarter notes and is relatively easy. The second solo is a bit more advanced due to the nearly constant eighth notes. Together they make a nice exercise in starting with a simple melody and then adding neighboring tones to make a more complex solo. Once you have two solos memorized you can combine the parts in different ways to make a third solo. You might start the third solo with the first part of solo two and then bring in the second part of solo one. Doing that is a good example of combining your musical vocabulary, repertoire, or phrases in different ways to come up with something new. ***Key of A.***

Footprints in the Snow

"Footprints in the Snow" was most famously recorded and performed by Bill Monroe. I guess by now you're getting the idea that Bill Monroe looms large in the legend of bluegrass and traditional country music. Did I say "looms large"? That's a criminal understatement! Bill Monroe invented bluegrass music! Not metaphorically, literally. On the way to doing that he invented a new style, or maybe several styles, of playing the mandolin. His importance to the music can't possibly be over-emphasized. If you want to understand the music and the role of the mandolin in this type of music, you need to listen to Bill.

This is not to say that you should flat out copy his playing and only play his style. He already did that and did it better than anyone else ever will. You should study his style, maybe copy it for a while, learn what makes it tick, and then use what you have learned to come up with your own style.

The first part of the "Footprints in the Snow" solo, the *verse*, played with single string 8th notes, sounds a bit like the traditional fiddle tune "Billy in the Lowground." You'll find a position change and a slide on beats 3 and 4 of measure 2. In measure 4, over the F chord, you'll add in some double stops. The double stops continue into the first measure of the first ending. On the last half of beat four in measure 4 you'll play a "lazy" double stop with your first finger. You can read more about this type of double stop on page 30 where it's included in the "Little Birdie" double stop solo. Following that you'll use your pinky to fret the first string, seventh fret B note.

The second part or *chorus* of the solo includes a lot of double stop tremolo notes. I thought this more stretched out, legato feel would make a nice contrast to the first part of the solo. You'll find another change up in measure 25 where you'll go back to single string quarter notes and eighth notes.

"Footprints in the Snow" has a long form, 32 measures, because it encompasses a verse and a chorus. You could think of it as a double solo. In performance you might want to split it up between two players, one playing the verse, one the chorus. Or, you could confine the solos to either the verse or the chorus.

As you play through the solo you'll notice that it's made up almost entirely of closed position, fretted notes. If you relocate the few open string notes to fretted closed position notes, you can move the solo to just about any key on the fingerboard. Give it a try! ***Key of C.***

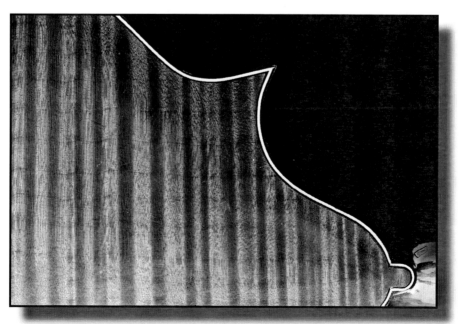

Back detail Schneider #49, 2005

Tracks 32 & 33

Footprints in the Snow

Arrangement © 2012 by Dix Bruce

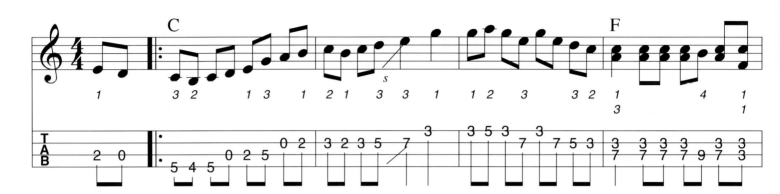

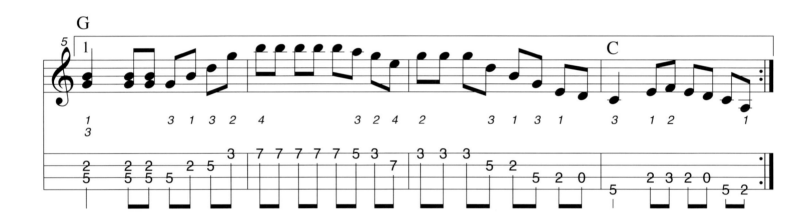

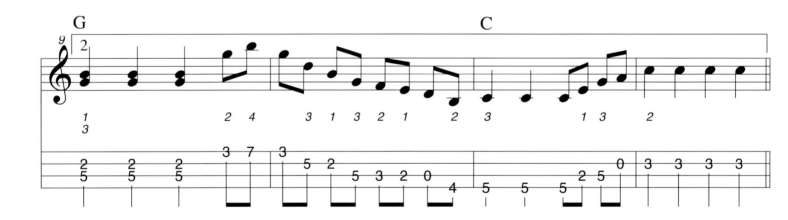

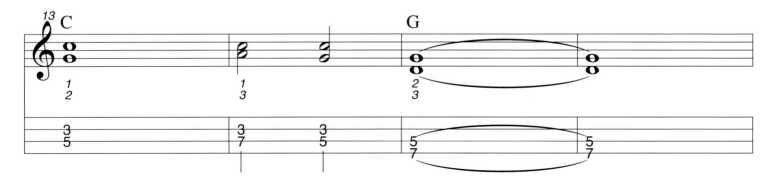

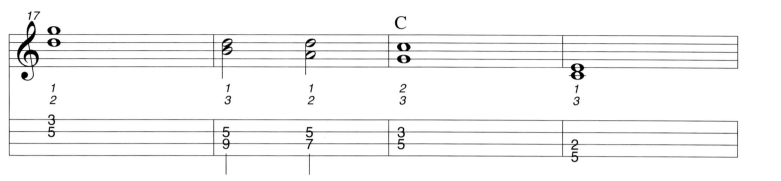

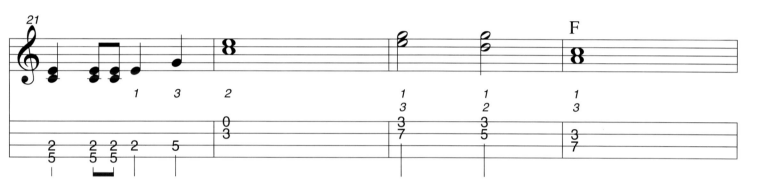

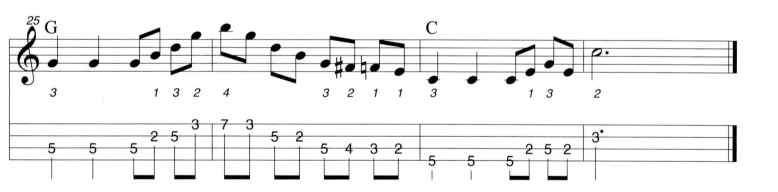

Going Down this Road Feeling Bad

This solo mixes quarter notes and half notes. I started the solo with the basic notes of the melody and then added in lots of neighboring tones. I also added in some chord arpeggios in measures 8 and 9. You'll find some blue notes in measures 10, 11, and 15, the B♭s, and another blue note, this time an F natural, in measure 14. *Key of G.*

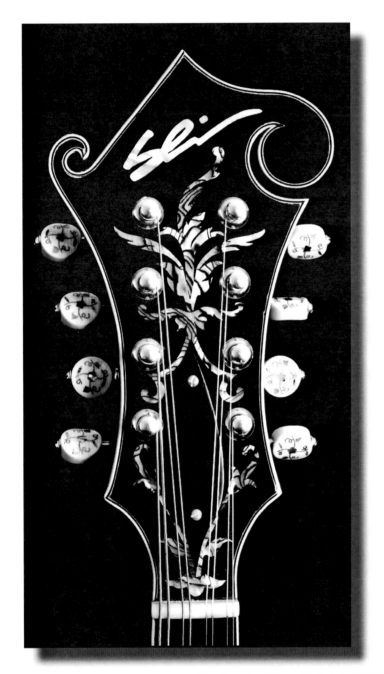 

Headstocks, Slikker F-5 style, 2009 (l.), BRW LP H3 mandolin, 2012 (r.)

Going Down this Road Feeling Bad

Arrangement © 2012 by Dix Bruce

All the Good Times are Past and Gone *arpeggio solo*

I love this song so much that I've written out about 20 different solos for it. Here's one that's written in the key of B♭. (Don't forget to try the back up part to "All the Good Times are Past and Gone" in the key of G on page 22.) In addition to being in a key that can seem scary if you're new to it, I structured the solo to deliberately be less melodic than most of the others in this book. This solo to "All the Good Times are Past and Gone" uses chord arpeggios as its main theme. To play an arpeggio you simply play each of the individual notes of a chord consecutively. Arpeggiating a chord is kind of the opposite of strumming it.

In my 20s I met and began playing with the great Frank Wakefield, an amazingly creative player and composer. Frank often composes solos based on arpeggios on a number of different songs. This solo is my attempt to sound a tiny bit like him. I hope you enjoy it.

Arpeggio-based solos can be adapted to hundreds and thousands of different songs. Their advantage is that they aren't melodic so they can be applied to an infinite number of melodies and chord progressions. I try to have a few arpeggio-based solos and passages in my repertoire at all times as they've come in handy on unfamiliar songs.

Don't let the key of B♭ throw you. In the final analysis all keys work the same way. This solo will help you scope out where the notes of the B♭ scale lie in this lower position on the fingerboard. I remember the time when I finally began to understand the concept of playing in any key. I was just beginning to peek into the alien worlds of keys like B♭, B natural, E♭, and A♭. When I finally gained a practical, working knowledge of these keys and how they fit together with all the other keys, I was elated. I felt liberated to be able to play in any key. With a little effort you'll be able to do the same thing.

Be sure to try lifting these chord arpeggios out of "All the Good Times are Past and Gone" and adapting them to the same chords in other 3/4 or waltz songs. You should also practice transposing the arpeggios to as many different chords and keys as you can so you can use them in any key. Don't forget to try them on songs in 4/4 time. You'll have to adapt the arpeggios to allow for the extra beat in every 4/4 measure. ***Key of B♭.***

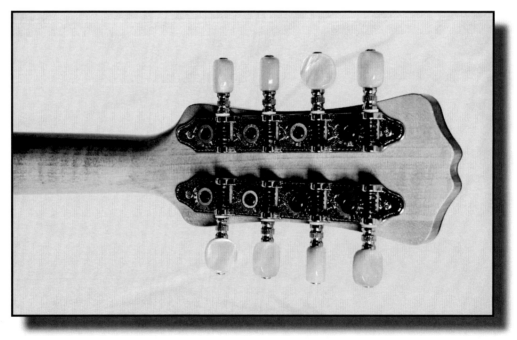

Headstock back detail Weber Bitterroot A, 2007

All the Good Times are Past and Gone *arpeggio solo*

Arrangement © 2012 by Dix Bruce

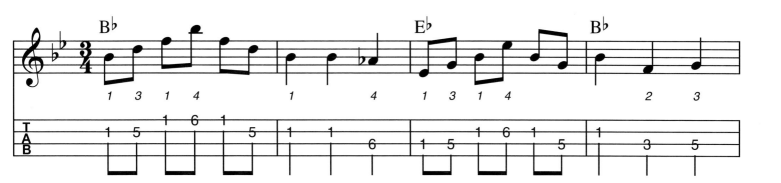

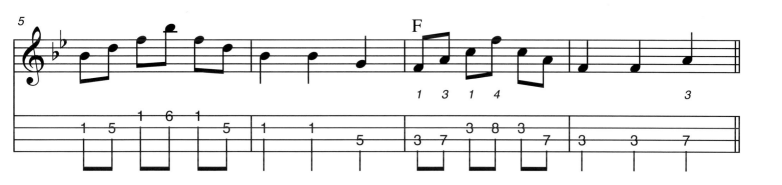

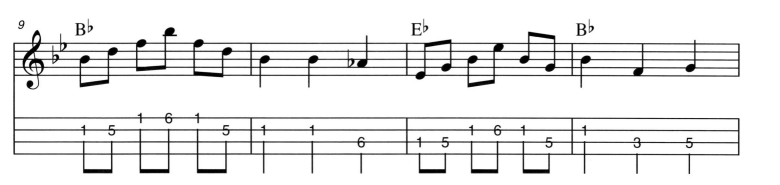

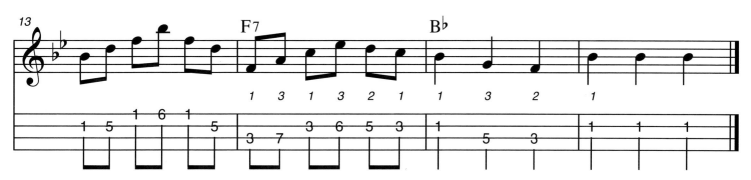

I am a Pilgrim

Arrangement © 2012 by Dix Bruce

This "I am a Pilgrim" solo is a straight forward, no nonsense, nothing fancy, single string solo with mixed fretted and open string notes. I play tremolo on notes longer than quarters. If you have difficulty with tremolo, leave it out for now.

With a little work you can turn this single string solo into a double stop solo. Without getting into too much detail, all you have to do is add the closest higher chord tone to the melody note. The difficult thing about it, especially if you're not used to the process, is that in order to play both tones at once you often have to move the open string note to a higher, closed position. Try it and see what you come up with. I'll post a double stop version on my website: http://www.musixnow.com/plpmandosolos.html. ***Key of G.***

Angel Band *double stop solo*

Here's a double stop tremolo solo to "Angel Band." The main differences between this solo and the back up part to "Angel Band" on page 24 are that this solo is melodic where the back up part was deliberately not melodic. Also, the solo is written here in the key of C while the back up part is in the key of G. It's incredibly important for you to eventually be able to play any song in any key. With a little effort you can make it happen.

As a side bar I should mention that the typical male vocal key for "Angel Band" is often the key of G. The typical female vocal key is C. If you learn both the solo and the back up part in both keys you'll be able to accommodate quite a range of singers, at least on this song.

Like the back up part, this "Angel Band" solo is built around double stop tremolo. Use tremolo on notes longer than quarters. Since the solo is made up of mixed half and quarter notes you'll need to practice starting and stopping your tremolo. The difficulty lies in starting and stopping your tremolo cleanly and in time. It's another necessary skill that every mandolinist will want to develop.

Another of the possible difficulties with playing this solo is to deftly move double stops around the fingerboard, especially in the quarter note passages in measures 22, 25, 26, 30, 33 and 34. Pay particular attention to the suggested fretting finger numbers shown below the standard notation. They'll help you figure it all out. And, as always, take it very slow until you teach your brain and your fingers how to work together. ***Key of C.***

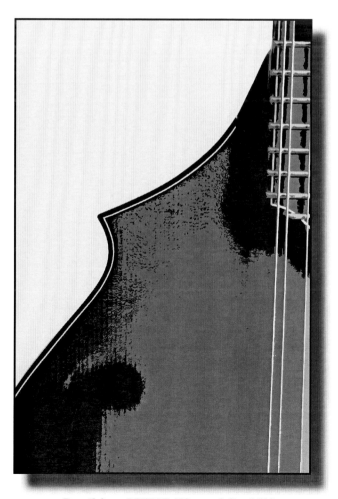

Detail from BRW LP H3 mandolin, 2012

Angel Band *double stop solo*

Arrangement © 2012 by Dix Bruce

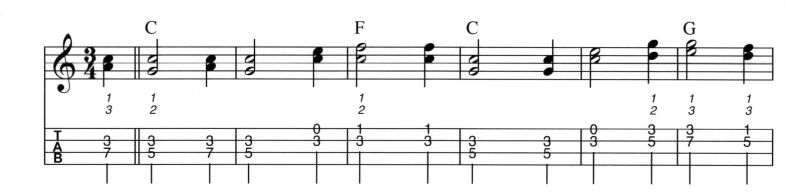

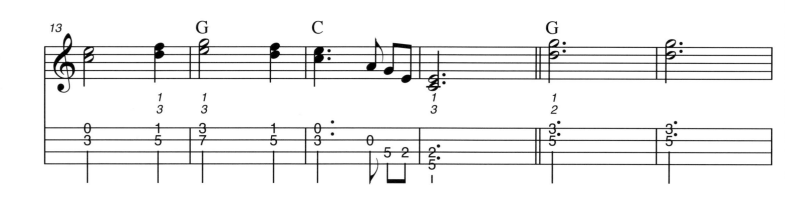

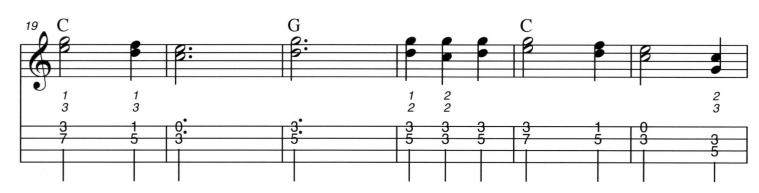

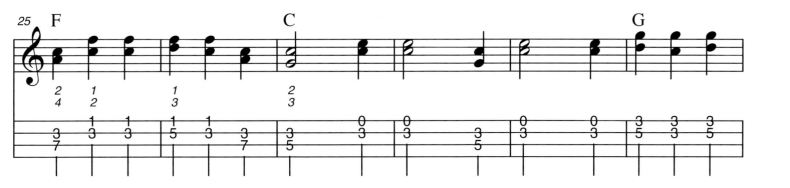

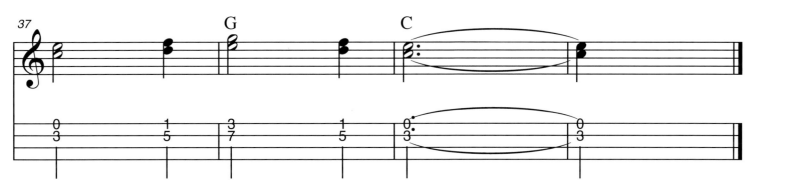

Banks of the Ohio *crosspicking solo*

As a beginning or intermediate mandolin player you've probably heard about the *crosspicking* technique on the mandolin. This "Banks of the Ohio" solo will give you a chance to try it out. Don't forget to learn the basic solo to "Banks of the Ohio" on page 20 before you try the crosspicking.

Jesse McReynolds, of the bluegrass brother duet Jim and Jesse, is the king of crosspicking on the mandolin. I interviewed him in the early 1980s and he told me that his inspiration for crosspicking on the mandolin came from the sound of the five string banjo roll. Jesse's playing is far faster and much more intricate than this "Banks of the Ohio" solo. If you listen to Jesse you'll know exactly what I'm talking about! But you have to start somewhere and "Banks of the Ohio" will give you a rewarding introduction to the style.

To play this crosspicking version of "Banks of the Ohio" we're going to set up a pattern on strings 4-2-3 or 3-1-2. We'll generally play the melody on the lowest and first string we play. The other two notes will be drone notes. At certain points in the solo (measure 2, the second half of measure 4, and elsewhere) we won't be able to play the full three string pattern because the melody is made up of shorter notes. Here we'll play a two note, two string pattern: one melody note plus one drone note.

As you hold a basic chord position with your fretting hand fingers you'll move in, out, and around that position to reach the melody and drone notes. In some cases you'll only have one fretted note that defines the chord. The sound of this solo is built around the use of the open E string over the D chord as in measures 1, 7, and 13. Theoretically speaking, the E note is the 9th tone relative to the D chord. Including the E turns the D chord into a D9. I just love that sound, but if you don't, all you have to do to change it to a regular D chord is to fret the first string, second fret F# note and substitute that note in for all the open string Es.

Pick directions and using the correct fretting finger numbers on the three string patterns are crucial. I suggest a down stroke on the first note and up strokes on the two following drone notes. It's a fairly natural motion given the layout of the pattern. In those passages with the two note pattern you'll play alternating down and up strokes. After you learn a few crosspicking solos you'll find that you don't have to think much about pick directions. For now though, I've marked them in the music above the tablature line. Down strokes are indicated by the down arrows, up strokes by the up arrows.

Try to play the pattern with very even time. Take it super slow at first and work toward setting up an even roll to float your melody and drone notes on. If you get some thuddy or buzzy notes, especially at first, don't worry about it and concentrate more on the flow of the roll.

Other than the challenge of crosspicking, the solo is fairly simple and straight forward. In measure 4 you'll be fretting both the fourth string, second fret A note and the third string second fret E note with your fourth finger. If you find it too difficult to fret both notes with one finger, use fingers one and two. ***Key of D.***

Tracks 42 & 43

Banks of the Ohio *crosspicking solo*

Arrangement © 2012 by Dix Bruce

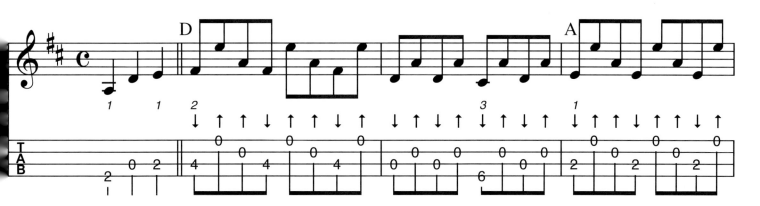

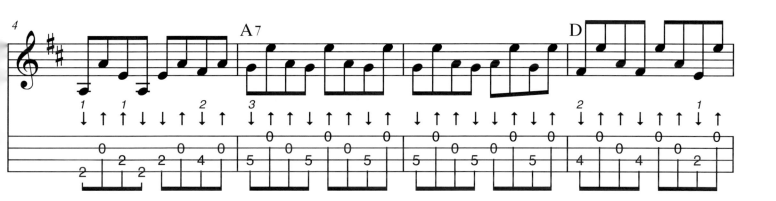

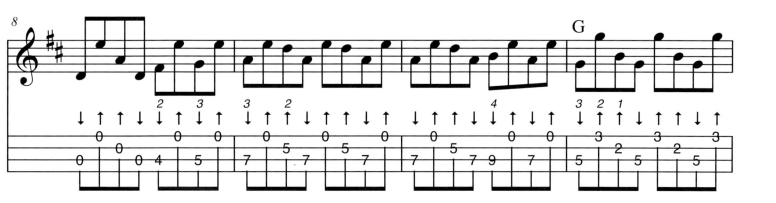

*Alt: Repeat previous
measure to overlap
next solo or verse then
ease back into rhythm*

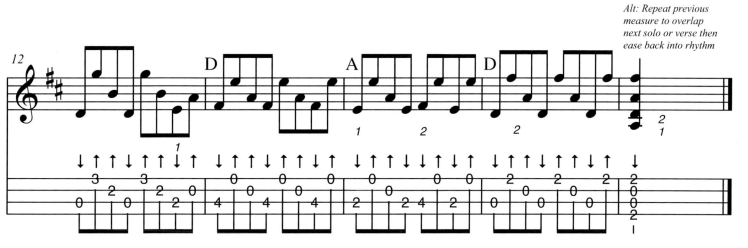

In the Pines

Arrangement © 2012 by Dix Bruce

This solo on "In the Pines" combines several of the techniques you've already been working with in this book including single note playing (throughout), blues notes (measures 6, 7, 14, 15), and double stop and double stop tremolo notes (measures 9 – 14). Use tremolo on notes longer than quarters. Try composing solos on this and other songs with just single string notes, just double stops, and many more blue notes. ***Key of G.***

Keep on the Sunny Side of Life

Here's another classic song from the movie "O Brother, Where Art Thou?" "Keep on the Sunny Side of Life" was originally recorded by the Carter Family in the 1920s and it became their theme song and a country hit along the way. It's another great song that you'll run into again and again.

The form of the solo is long, just like the song "Footprints in the Snow" (page 35) with a verse, measures 1 through 16, and a chorus, measures 17 through 32. You could play the whole form as a solo but you might want to split it up between two players, one playing the first part or verse, one playing the second part or chorus.

The solo is written in a closed G major scale position up the fingerboard. If you're not used to playing up in that region of the fingerboard this solo may be challenging for you, at least at first. The most difficult parts are probably those where you have to use your fourth finger in measures 9, 11, 16, 21, 22, and 29. Just about everyone's tendency is to rush through these parts and, as a result, the notes get sloppy. Once again, take it slow until you teach that pinky what you want it to do. Developing a strong and useful fourth finger can be one of the most daunting physical challenges for a mandolinist to master. We all have trouble with it. That little finger just does not want to behave! However, I can tell you this from personal experience: once you tame it, even a little bit, you'll be able to play ever more advanced passages easily.

Watch for one difficult fretting finger move in measures 13 and 14. There you'll have to use your first fretting finger to play two different consecutive notes on the same string. The passage starts on the last half of the fourth beat in measure 13 where you'll play the third string, fifth fret G. Following that, on the first half of the first beat in measure 14, you'll play the third string, fourth fret F#. You'll have to shift your whole fretting hand a bit to make it work. ***Key of G.***

Detail from Kentucky KM-1000 early 1980s

Keep on the Sunny Side of Life

Arrangement © 2012 by Dix Bruce

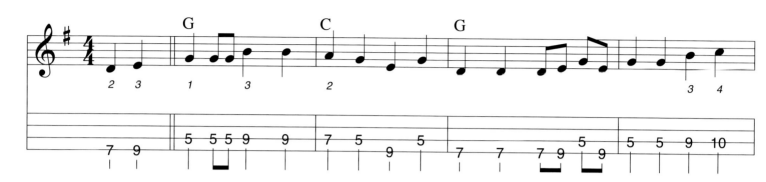

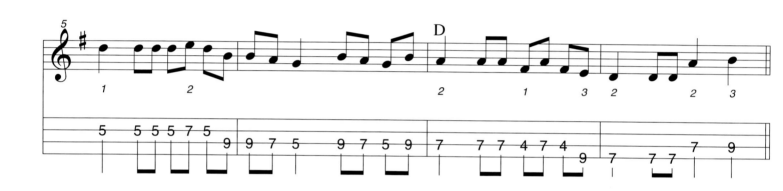

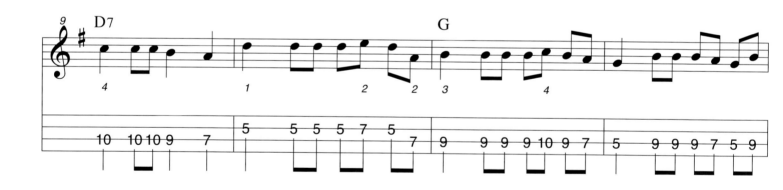

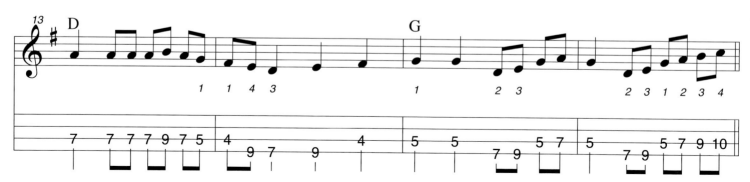

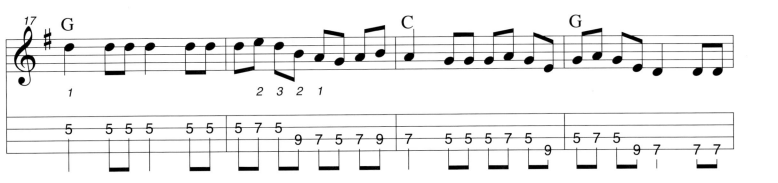

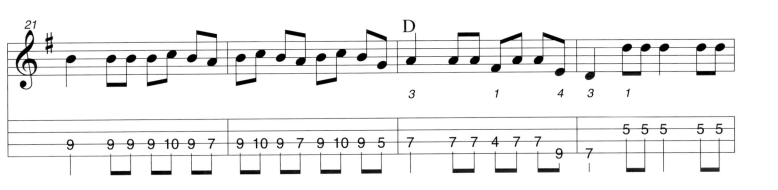

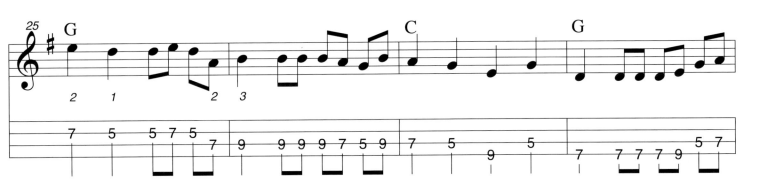

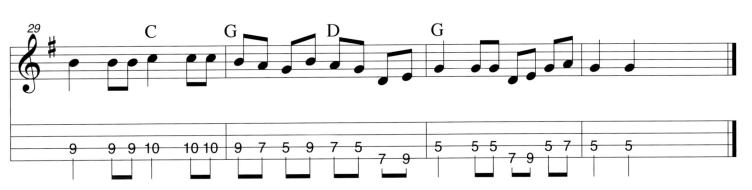

Little Maggie

Arrangement © 2012 by Dix Bruce

Another of the greatest hits of bluegrass, "Little Maggie" is a must-know song. This solo, with its slightly unusual blue notes and its closed position placement on the fingerboard, make it somewhat more difficult than some of the solos in this book. That said I hope you'll give it a try no matter where you are on the developmental level.

You'll use nearly continual down-up picking to play all the eighth notes in this solo. It's very much in the early bluegrass/Bill Monroe style but the modal chord movement, back and forth between the tonalities of the key of A and G, plus some added blue notes, give the solo a real bluesy feel. ***Key of A.***

Lord, I'm Coming Home

Here's a closed position double stop tremolo solo on the beautiful old song "Lord, I'm Coming Home." You'll probably want to tremolo notes longer than quarters but I often keep my tremolo rolling pretty much through the whole solo. Normally you'd start and stop your tremolo to articulate the changing notes and double stops. That can make the solo choppy. Try it both ways: with continuous tremolo and with tremolo mainly on notes longer than quarters.

You'll want to pay close attention to the suggested fretting finger numbers. Try to memorize the solo and then move it up and down the fingerboard to various other keys. Move it up three frets to the key of B♭. If this new key gives you trouble, you can download the music from my website: http://www.musixnow.com/plpmandosolos. html. ***Key of G.***

Headstock detail, front and back, Gibson A-model, early 1920s

Lord, I'm Coming Home

Arrangement © 2012 by Dix Bruce

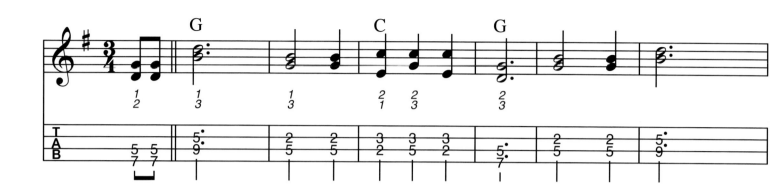

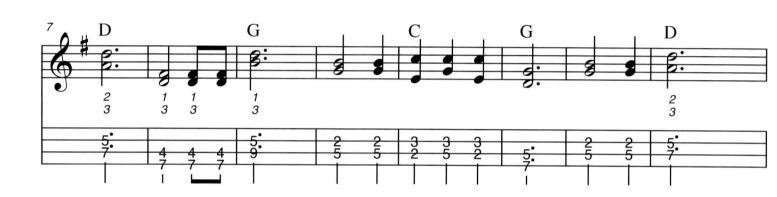

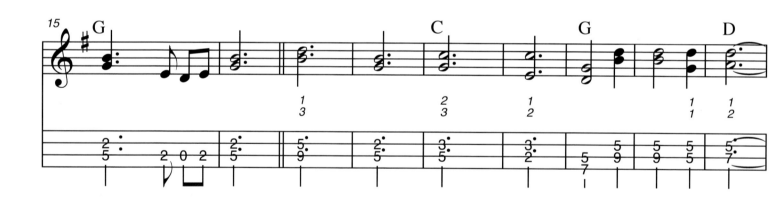

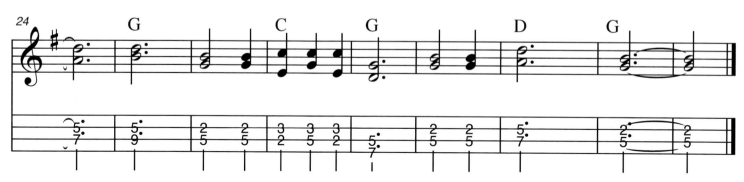

Man of Constant Sorrow

This solo to "Man of Constant Sorrow," yet another great song from the movie "O Brother, Where Art Thou?" mixes quarter and eighth note passages with blue notes and slides. You can identify the blues notes, flatted third and seventh tones of the D scale, by looking for the natural accidental signs in the standard notation making the F♯ (third) and C♯ (seventh) into F♮ (flatted third) and C♮ (flatted seventh). It'll work the same way in every key. Just find the notes in the standard music notation that have accidentals (flats or naturals, possibly sharps) added. If these notes are the third or seventh of the major scale, they'll be blue notes.

Most of the eighth note passages will be played with continuous up-down picking. I usually slide into the notes identified with a small "s" by starting about two frets below the fret I want to slide up to. In measure 11 you'll slide up to the third string, seventh fret A note and then immediately play another A but this time on the open second string.

As you can see from the tablature, this solo has several open string notes. Try moving the solo across the fingerboard. Will that work? No, because the solo spans all four strings. If you move it across the fingerboard to either a higher or lower key you'll run out of places to play some of the notes. If you want to transpose this solo you'll have to relocate the open string notes to higher, fretted positions and move the whole solo up the fingerboard. If that's difficult or doesn't work, feel free to change any notes that are problematic. *Key of D.*

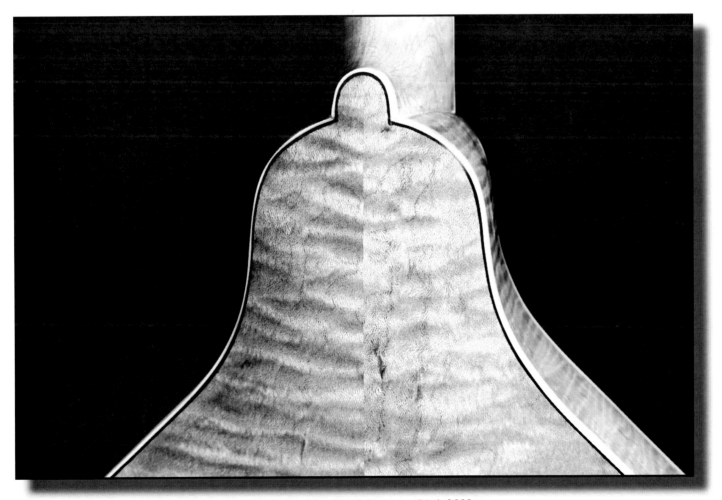

Back shoulder detail, Pomeroy PA 4, 2008

Man of Constant Sorrow

Arrangement © 2012 by Dix Bruce

Molly and Tenbrooks

"Molly and Tenbrooks" is another bluegrass and Bill Monroe classic. If you play bluegrass for any length of time, you'll play this song.

Bill Monroe performed a lot of songs in the key of B. Modern bluegrass musicians have followed his lead and often also play in the key of B. To give you experience in those environs, I wrote this "Molly and Tenbrooks" solo in the key of B.

If you're not used to playing in B, it can throw you for a loop. It sure flummoxed me when I first attempted it. With a little practice though, I began to see that the key of B works just like any other key, especially in the closed position. This solo uses a B major scale position. The root note, the B, is played on the second string, second fret B with your index finger. This is the same closed scale position you've used on several other solos in this book like "Little Birdie," (page 28) "Down in the Valley to Pray," (page 32) "Keep on the Sunny Side" (page 49) and there'll be many more. The only difference is that here we're in the key of B.

Most of the notes of the solo will come from one octave of the B scale. I say "most" because you'll also use a couple of notes, the F♯ and G♯ on the third string, fourth and sixth frets. The F♯ is the lower fifth of the B major scale. The G♯ is the lower sixth.

Since the solo is written in a closed position, you can move it around the fingerboard relatively easily to different keys. Be sure to practice doing that. Memorize the solo before you attempt to move it. That'll make your efforts much easier. First try moving the whole solo up by one half step. Your first notes will be on string three, frets 5 and 7 and you'll be playing the solo in the key of C. Once you can do that, move the solo up to as many other keys as you can reach. Can you move the original solo down one fret from the key of B to the key of B♭?

You can also move this solo **over** the fingerboard to a new key. Notice that the tablature numbers span three strings: 3, 2, and 1. You can move this solo to a lower set of three strings by starting it on string 4, frets 4 and 6. What new key will you be in? Can you move this new position up and down the fingerboard to different keys? Email me if you can't figure it out: dix@musixnow.com. ***Key of B.***

Molly and Tenbrooks

Arrangement © 2012 by Dix Bruce

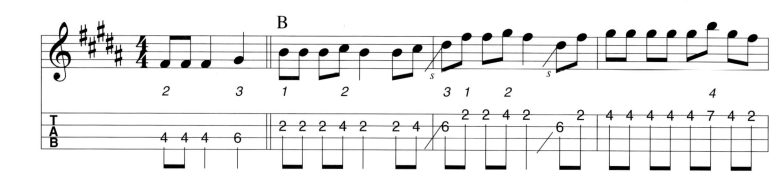

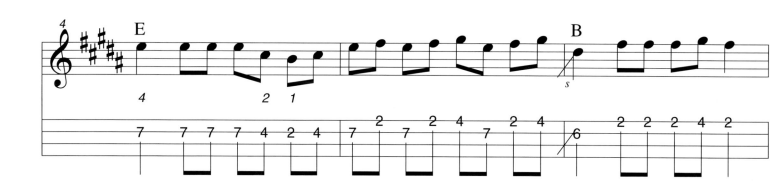

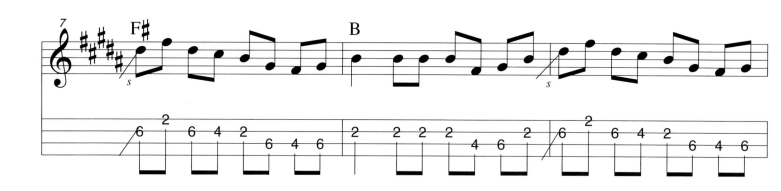

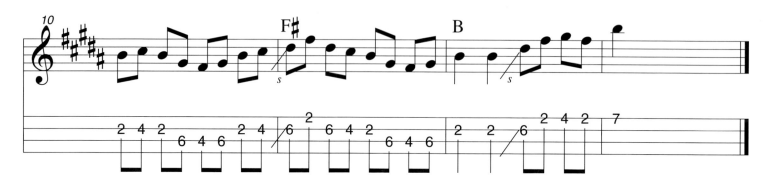

F-5 style mandolin by Annette Slikker, 2009

Tracks 56 & 57

Precious Memories

Arrangement © 2012 by Dix Bruce

I love this song. It's a beautiful melody with incredibly moving lyrics. Many people think of it as a gospel song but it's really just a song about remembering old times and loved ones who have passed away.

The solo to "Precious Memories" is written in two parts. The first sixteen measures are the verse, the second sixteen are the chorus. As with a few other long form, verse/chorus solos in this book, you can play the whole thing or either part as the solo. (Pages 35, 49, 45, 67, 75, and 83.)

"Precious Memories" uses tremolo throughout. By this point in the book you know that I generally suggest tremolo on notes longer than quarters. In the verse you'll be playing all single string notes. I added a few hammer ons noted in the music with a small "*h*." The great mandolinist Jethro Burns used to refer to this type of hammer on as a "Kramer lick" named after the equally great Nashville pianist Floyd Kramer.

The chorus or second part of the solo builds a bit in intensity with the addition of double stops played with tremolo. The suggested fretting finger numbers will help you locate them correctly.

The solo is played in a closed position, and, like many closed position solos in this book, it works out of a closed G major scale position with the root or first G note played on the third string, fifth fret, with the first finger. When you're comfortable playing it as written in the key of G, be sure to try moving it around the fingerboard to different keys. ***Key of G.***

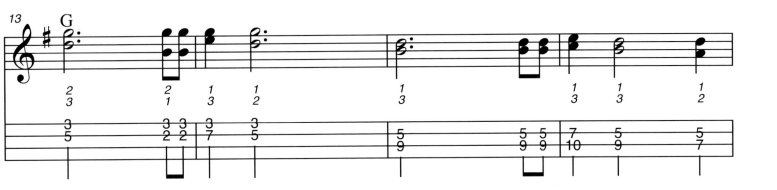

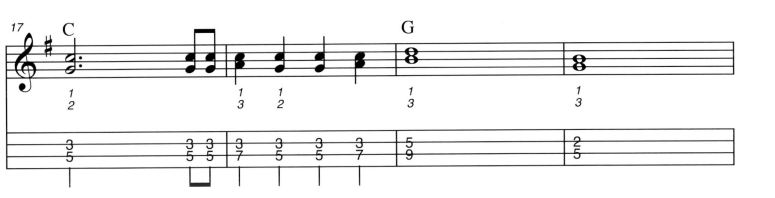

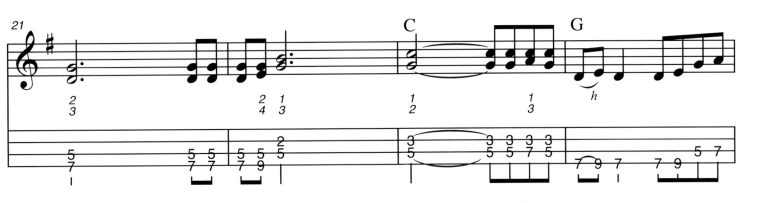

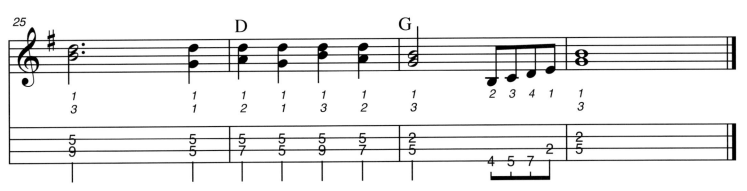

Pretty Polly

"Pretty Polly" is a traditional song that has been recorded again and again by many artists. Ralph Stanley's version is probably the best known for its stark, haunting tone. I tried to capture some of that quality in this solo by using lots of blue notes (flatted thirds and fifths) to give the solo a modal sound. Blue notes sound the way they do because they temporarily pull the sound of the solo from its home tonality, the key of G, down to the key of F.

The solo is made up of all single string notes (no double stops), includes some open string notes, and spans all four strings. You'll have to relocate or change these open string notes if you want to move the solo to different keys. The solo also includes several hammer ons and slides.

Julie Cline and I recorded a version of "Pretty Polly" based on this solo. It's on our "Look at it Rain" CD which is available on my website: http://www.musixnow.com, from iTunes, and from CD Baby. *Key of G.*

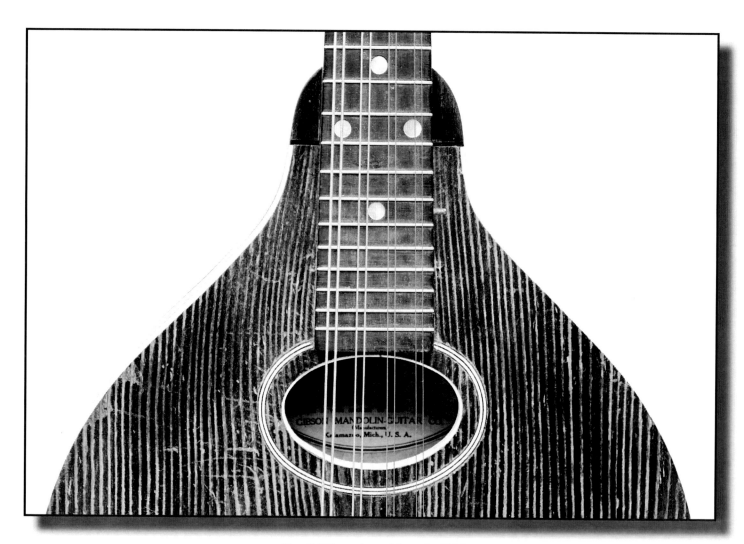

Detail Gibson A-model, early 1920s

Pretty Polly

Arrangement © 2012 by Dix Bruce

Hills of Roane County *double stop tremolo back up part*

Arrangement © 2012 by Dix Bruce

Let's look at two different ways to play back up mandolin behind the vocal on the song "Hills of Roane County." Whenever you play a back up part behind a vocal it's important to remember that your playing must support the singer and not compete with or cover what they're doing. Your mission is to enhance the vocal and make the whole performance sound better.

The first back up part to "Hills of Roane County" is in the double stop tremolo style. It'll make a very pretty instrumental pad that the vocal can float over. Be sure to play it quietly and sensitively.

Once you can play the part as written, try lifting out different chord passages and applying them to other songs in the key of G and in 3/4 or waltz time. You should also practice moving this part up and down the fingerboard to different keys. You'll find it to be relatively easy since it's written in a closed position without any open string notes. A "call and response" back up part follows on page 65. ***Key of G.***

Hills of Roane County *call and response back up part*

Here's another style of back up for "Hills of Roane County." The melody to "Hills of Roane County," like a lot of songs in traditional folk and bluegrass genre, is made up of several short notes followed by a longer held note. The mandolin, or any other instrument for that matter, can play a phrase to fill in behind these long, held notes. The effect is a kind of a call and response between the vocalist and whatever instrument is backing up the vocal. We'll refer to this back up approach as "call and response."

To perform it you'll wait for the vocalist to sing a phrase and then you'll fill whatever space is left. When you're not playing you can either rest or strum back up chords as you normally would. You could also combine this back up part with the previous and play tremolo double stops behind the vocal. Since most of the back up licks end on dotted half notes, which are held for three beats, you could either tremolo these notes or pick them and let them ring. The possibilities are endless. Listen to musicans you admire and see how they back up vocalists. The most important thing, and I can't stress this enough, is to support the vocal. Again, be careful not to cover it up or compete with it. Be concious of how the whole band sounds and help make the vocal the center of attention.

All of the back up licks below are built around chord apreggios. As you might expect, you can lift these licks out of the back up part and apply them to any similar song in 3/4 or waltz time. Some of the licks are in closed positions and you can move these up and down the fingerboard to different chords in different keys. Other licks have open string notes in them. You can move these across the fingerboard to separate sets of strings and use them on different chords and in different keys. ***Key of G.***

Headstock detail Gilchrist F-5, 2000

Hills of Roane County *call and response back up part*

Arrangement © 2012 by Dix Bruce

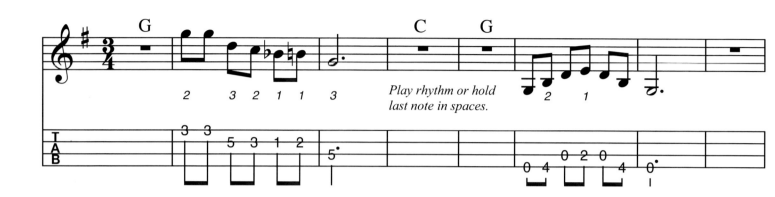

*Play rhythm or hold
last note in spaces.*

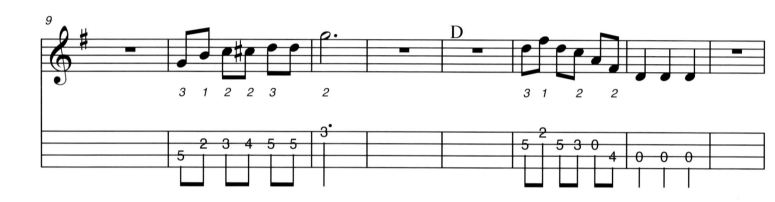

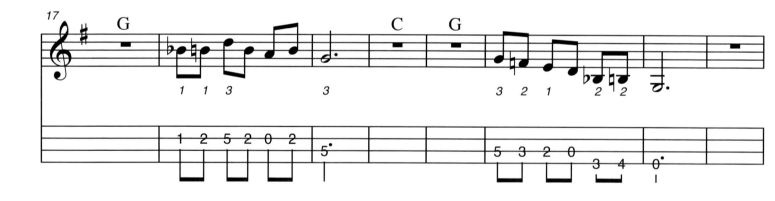

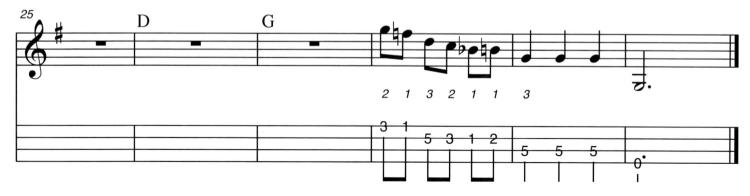

Red Wing

Arrangement © 2012 by Dix Bruce

"Red Wing" is a popular song from the early part of the last century. It's most often performed as an instrumental, usually in the key of G or C. This solo is in the key of C.

The solo takes the basic melody of "Red Wing" and adds in neighboring tones, mostly eighth notes. It makes for a good case study of that type of note fill-in solo composition. You can find the basic, unadorned melody the solo is based on in my "Parking Lot Picker's Songbooks." The solo includes some open string notes that you'll have to change if you want to move it to different keys. Since the solo spans three strings, you can move it over one string to strings, 3, 2, and 1. Your first note will be an open third string D instead of the open fourth string G. The new location will transpose the solo to the key of G. This will allow you to play "Red Wing" in both of the most performed keys, C and G.

I've mentioned the importance of listening to other players, not just mandolin players. It's very useful to know and understand how other players handle musical situations that you'll encounter. As you listen you'll be learning and collecting. You might not even be aware of it as it happens.

For example, I just realized that the basic idea for this "Red Wing" solo dates from the fall of 1973. A few of my friends and I drove from Madison, WI, to a bluegrass festival in Port Huron, MI. It was a long haul but we got to see and hear Ralph Stanley and the Clinch Mountain Boys and also Larry Sparks and the Lonesome Ramblers, among other wonderful bands. Both the Stanley and Sparks bands featured exquisite lead guitar playing like I'd never heard before. I was inspired by that new and beautiful sound. I remember that Larry Sparks played "Red Wing" as a guitar feature on his show. It blew me away. As luck would have it, Larry had recorded "Red Wing" on his "Ramblin' Guitar" instrumental LP and I was able to buy a copy. As soon as I got home I studied that recording and learned to play "Red Wing," on the guitar. When I began to play "Red Wing," on the mandolin, try as I might, the mandolin would play nothing but the same basic guitar arrangement I'd learned from Larry Sparks. Over the years both guitar and mandolin versions have changed and evolved but I still remember that Larry Sparks' seed of inspiration led to both. So keep listening, learning, collecting. You just never know what'll stick or what'll become a valuable and treasured part of your own repertoire.

The form of "Red Wing" includes a verse (the first 16 measures) and a chorus (the next 16 measures). You could play the whole form as a solo or split it with another player. ***Key of C.***

Red Wing

Arrangement © 2012 by Dix Bruce

Tracks 64 & 65

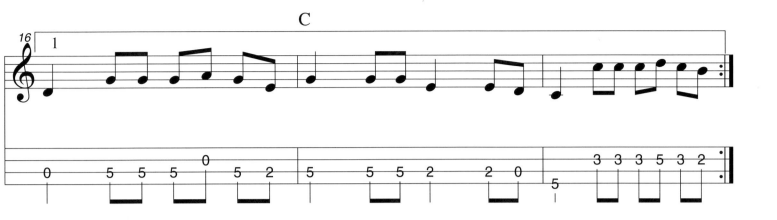

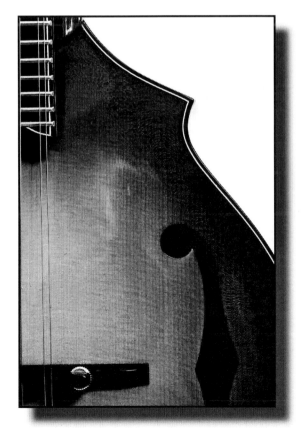

Front detail BRW LP H3 mandolin, 2012

Little Sadie

Arrangement © 2012 by Dix Bruce

This solo to "Little Sadie" is quite simple and made up of a mixture of quarter and eighth notes. If there's a difficult passage it's in measures 13 through 15 where you'll play continuous up and down picked eighth notes.

There's one slide in measure 5. See if you can add a few more slides here and there to make the solo a little more complex. ***Key of Em.***

Will the Circle be Unbroken?

Of all the songs you should know in order to play bluegrass-old-time-folk-country music "Will the Circle be Unbroken" is probably number one on the list. This song is played constantly! The solo is written in a closed, mostly double stop position out of the G major scale. The solo is in a closed position because I'm sure you'll need to transpose it to other keys to accommodate different vocal ranges. Everybody sings "Will the Circle be Unbroken"!

As you've already done with many solos in this book, start by planting your first finger on the third string, fifth fret G note. You'll stay in this position for most, but not all, of the solo. You'll shift position when you get to measure 5 over the C chord, in measure 11 over the G chord, and also in measure 14 over the D chord.

You'll use the "lazy" double stop, where you play both notes with your first finger, in measures 1, 2, 3, 9, 10, etc. When you use the "lazy" double stop you're playing an interval of a fifth. You can substitute a different double stop, one with an interval of a third, by shifting positions more frequently. To do that, play a G note with your third finger on the third string, fifth fret and your first finger on the second string, second fret B.

This solo to "Will the Circle be Unbroken" has only one open string note, the final open fourth string G in the last measure. If you change that note and move it up an octave to the third string, fifth fret, played with your first finger, you'll have a solo played completely in a closed position. That will allow you to move the solo up and down the fingerboard to many different keys. Be sure to try it. You can download a version of this solo in the key of F from my website: http://www.musixnow.com/plpmandosolos.html. ***Key of G.***

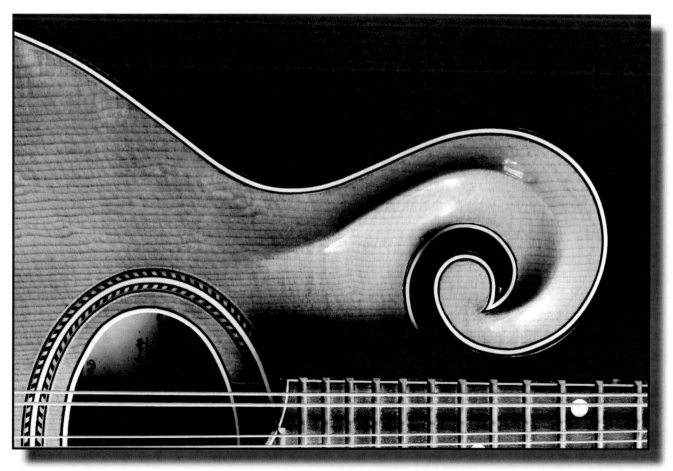

Curl and soundhole detail, Schneider mandolin, 2005

Will the Circle be Unbroken?

Arrangement © 2012 by Dix Bruce

Tracks 68 & 69

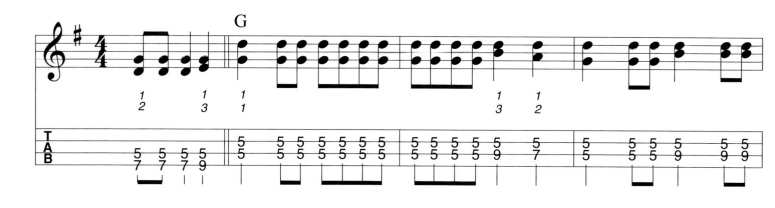

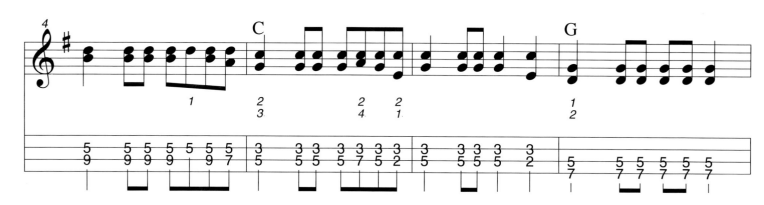

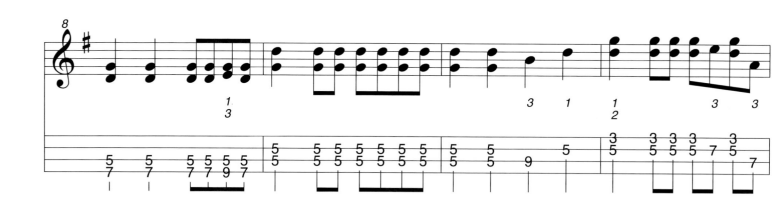

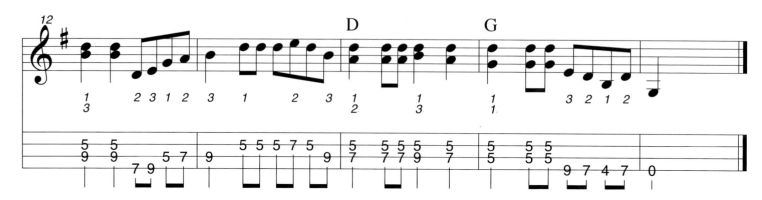

Reuben's Train

These days "Reuben's Train" is usually performed as an instrumental but it does have mysterious and memorable, if somewhat confusing, lyrics. I included them in my "Parking Lot Picker's Songbooks."

"Reuben's Train" is known by a variety of names, "Reuben," "Lonesome Reuben," and "Train 45" among them. It's a favorite of guitarists and banjo players and if you play with either, you'll probably run into this tune sooner or later.

The solo is written in closed position with no open string notes. That means that you can move it relatively easily to different keys up or down the fingerboard. Just keep the relative distances of the notes, one from another, intact as you move it. Since the solo spans three strings, 2, 3, and 4, you can move it over one string, higher in pitch, to strings 1, 2, 3. Your first note will be the third string, seventh fret A note instead of the fourth string seventh fret D note. What will your new key be? Hint: the original solo is in the key of D. Its first note is a D. If the relocated solo starts on an A note, what's your best guess as to the new key?

You'll play a number of nice slides and hammer ons in "Reuben's Train." If you have difficulty playing them, leave them out at first. Be sure to add them back in eventually as they'll make the solo much richer and more interesting.

This solo defines and maps out a different basic fretting hand position than we've used so far in this book. I've talked a lot about the major scale position with the root played with the first finger. In this case, the root, D, will be played by the third finger on the fourth string, seventh fret. Your other fretting hand fingers will be applied accordingly. The addition of all the blue notes changes the sound of the major scale significantly.

You'll encounter some challenging stretches between the first and fourth fretting fingers in measures 8, 12, and 15. You'll stretch between the seventh fret D note (fourth finger) and the second fret A note (first finger).

If you take the solo apart you'll be able to isolate quite a number of bluesy licks that you can lift out of this song and adapt to many others in any key. Give it a try! *Key of D.*

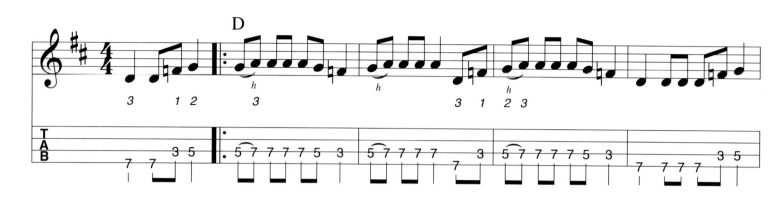

Reuben's Train

Arrangement © 2012 by Dix Bruce

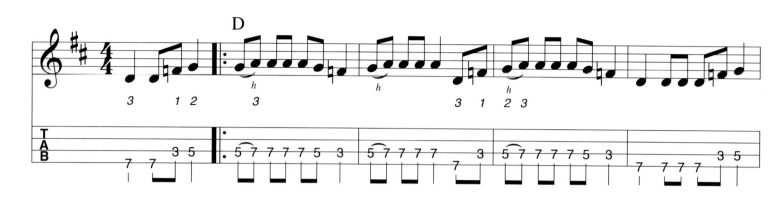

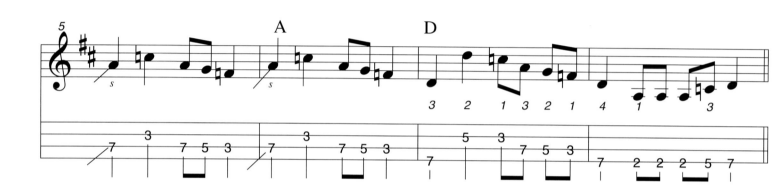

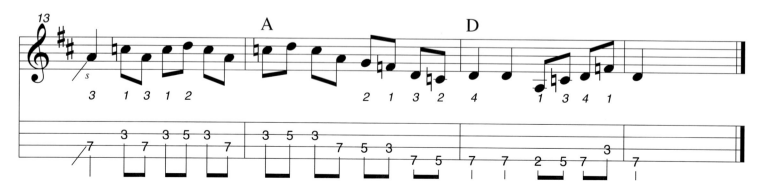

The Wayfaring Stranger

Arrangement © 2012 by Dix Bruce

"The Wayfaring Stranger" is a haunting and beautiful melody that makes a wonderful solo mandolin piece. Most of the solo is played with double stops. Many of them are very long, legato notes. You'll get the chance to express a lot of emotion in this solo. You'll probably want to tremolo notes that are longer than quarters. Be sure to practice starting and stopping your tremolo as you'll need to be able to do that to transition between eighths and quarters to halves and tied wholes.

The notes of the solo span three strings, 1, 2 and 3. You can transpose the solo from the key of Em to the key of Am by simply moving it over one string. The first note in the new key will be the fourth string, second fret A note. If you keep the distances between all the notes relatively the same you should find the transposition quite easy to accomplish. The tablature numbers will be identical, just moved over one string.

"The Wayfaring Stranger" is another of the songs in this book with a long form made up of a verse, the first 16 measures, and a chorus, the second 16 measures. As I suggested elsewhere, you might want to split the form between two or more players. ***Key of Em.***

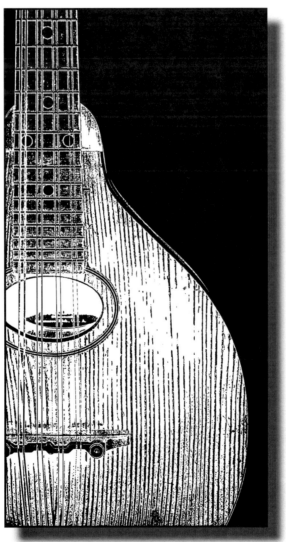

Gibson A-model, early 1920s

The Wayfaring Stranger

Arrangement © 2012 by Dix Bruce

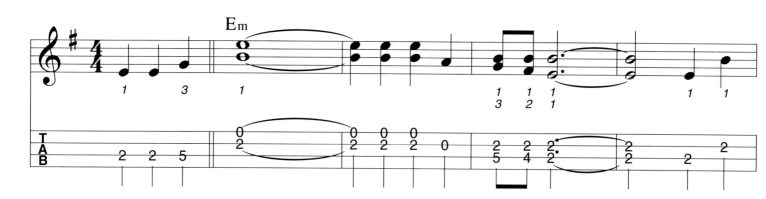

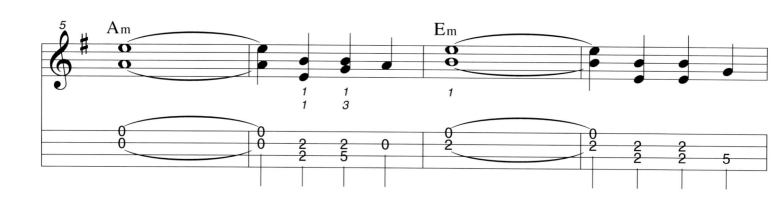

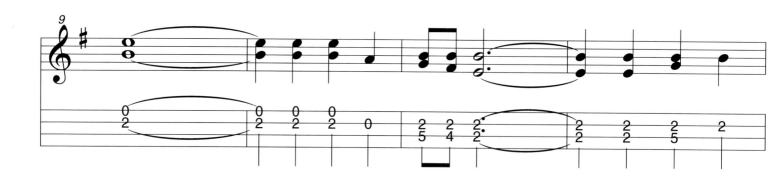

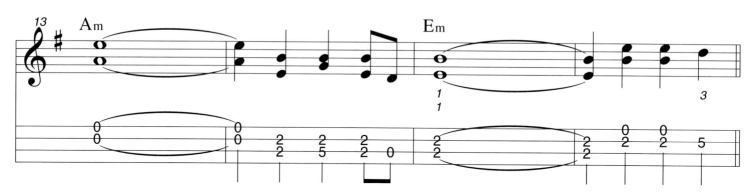

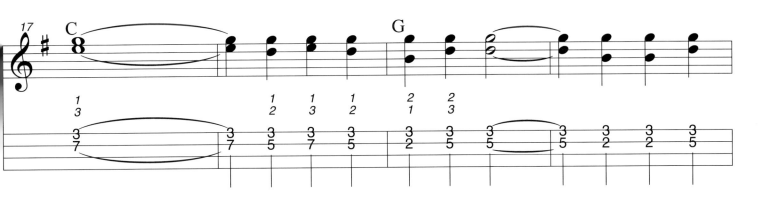

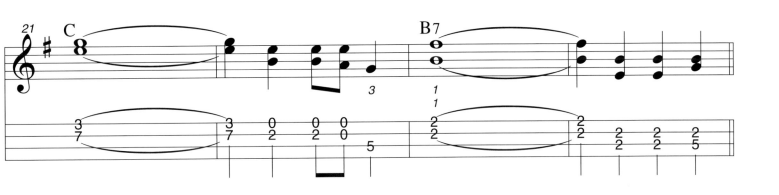

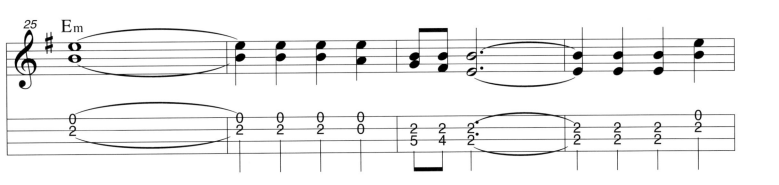

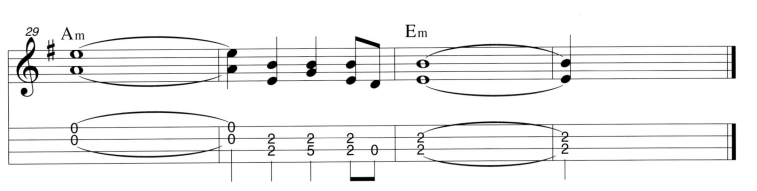

Roll in My Sweet Baby's Arms

Made famous by Lester Flatt and Earl Scruggs, "Roll in My Sweet Baby's Arms" is a bluegrass standard played all over the world. The solo is a relatively simple double stop arrangement with mixed fretted and open strings in the double stops. Beginners may have a bit of difficulty playing the continuous double stop eighth notes over two strings. As I always suggest, slow the solo down until you get the hang of it and then gradually speed it up.

The solo also contains a few slides. In measures 4 and 9 you'll slide into open string double stops. **Key of A.**

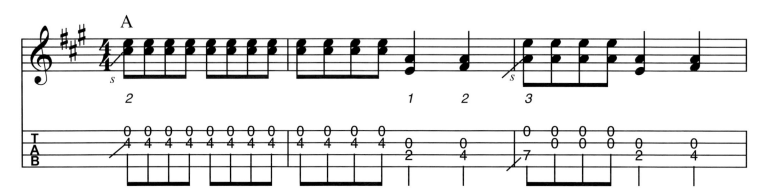

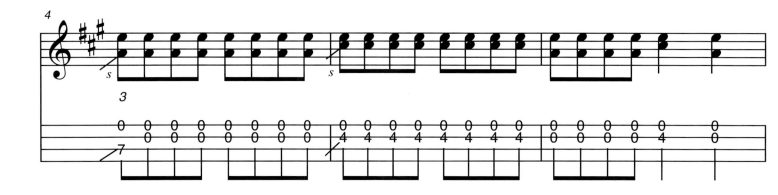

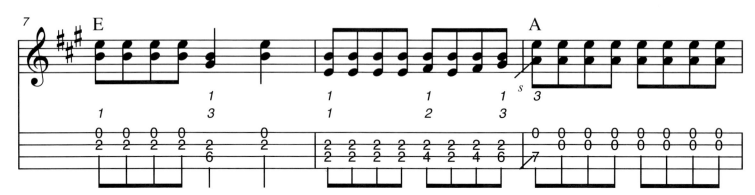

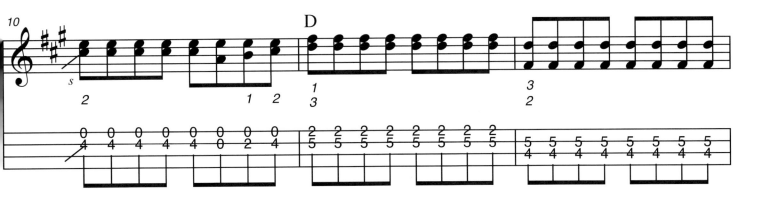

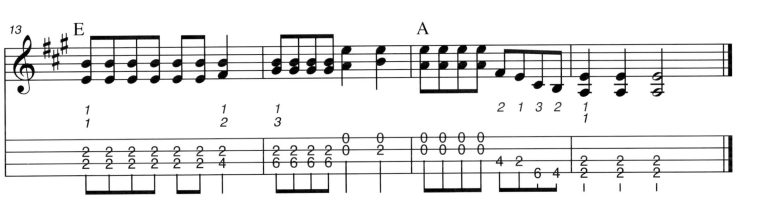

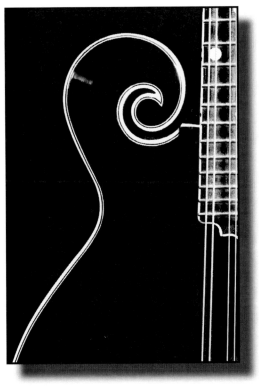

Detail from Kentucky KM-1000 early 1980s

There's More Pretty Girls Than One *single string solo*

I wrote out two solos, one on page 80 and the other on page 82, to "There's More Pretty Girls Than One." The first is a fairly straightforward statement of the melody. The second is a more abstract and less melodic solo based on chord arpeggios. Let's look at the melodic solo first.

The first solo starts out with a pickup of four eighth notes. After that you'll mix together quarter and eighth notes with several slides ("*s*") on quarter notes. The solo also mixes fretted and open string notes. It should be playable by advanced beginners and intermediate mandolinists though, not being in a closed position, it won't be easily moveable up or down the fingerboard to different keys.

Since the solo spans all four strings you can't easily or automatically move it across the fingerboard to any different keys. If you change the first string open E notes in measures 5 and 9 you can move this solo up in pitch and over a string by starting the pickup on the third string, second fret. How would you change those notes? First of all, you could just leave them out. Of course that would change the melody considerably. Or, you could play the first string open E notes on the second string, seventh fret. Use your fourth finger. Moving the solo in this way will transpose it from the key of D to the key of A. Give it a try. If you run into difficulty, you can download the music from my website: http://www.musixnow.com/plpmandosolos.html. ***Key of D.***

The second "There's More Pretty Girls Than One" solo is in an arpeggio style based on the notes of the chord across the fingerboard. I think of this style as Frank Wakefield-esque. I have been inspired by Frank's playing since the early 1970s. He's a technical master of many styles of playing and always says something unique with his music.

This "There's More Pretty Girls Than One" solo is made up mostly of eighth notes but has some quarters mixed in for variety's sake. To play a chord arpeggio we play the individual notes of a chord one after the other rather than strumming all the notes at once. This solo will help you locate different chord arpeggios around the fingerboard. All of them are played in closed positions and all begin with the root tone of whatever chord you're playing. They don't have to start with the root. You could also start the arpeggios on the third or fifth of the chord. In fact, you should practice doing that as a way to discover new ways to play these arpeggios. You may notice that all arpeggios I used in the solo ascend. You could also have them descend. Give it a go.

Measure 14 has a major fretting hand position shift and finger stretch. Take it slow at first and teach your fingers what they need to do.

As I mentioned, all of the individual arpeggios are in closed positions. You can pull any arpeggio out of this solo and apply it to another chord in a waltz or 3/4 song. You can also transpose the arpeggios to new chords by moving them up and down the fingerboard. As you play through the solo, hold your fretting hand in the chord shapes you're playing. That will make the solo about 100% easier. Really. Look for the chord shapes and try to relate the sound of what you're playing to the look and feel of your fretting hand. That will help you adapt this technique to other chords and songs.

Don't forget to try moving the whole solo to different keys. How about moving it up three frets to the key of F? How about moving the original solo down one fret to the key of D♭ or C#? I'll post both on my website (http://www.musixnow.com/plpmandosolos.html). Before you download them, take some time to struggle through the process. If you've never worked with this kind of transposition, it'll take a few tries to get it to click with your fingers and brain. If you don't try it on your own and build those brain/finger pathways, it'll be a lot more work in the long run. Once you get it, you'll have a much deeper understanding of how the mandolin works. Your playing will take a quantum leap. Give the transposition a shot on your own before you download. ***Key of D.***

There's More Pretty Girls Than One *single string solo*

Arrangement © 2012 by Dix Bruce

There's More Pretty Girls Than One *arpeggio solo*

Arrangement © 2012 by Dix Bruce

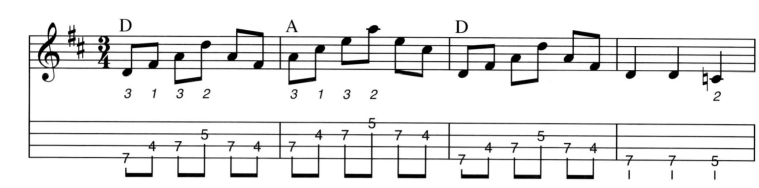

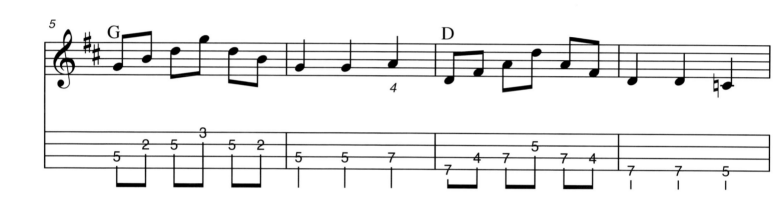

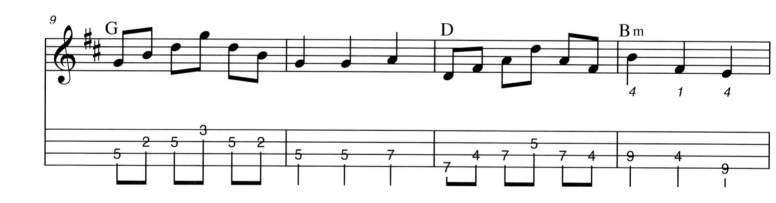

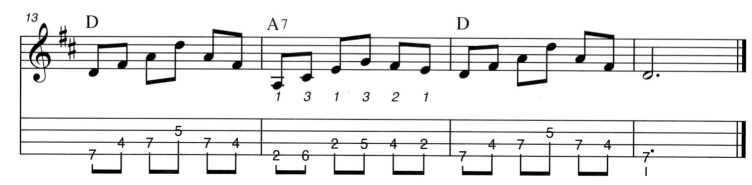

Down in the Willow Garden *crosspicking solo*

"Down in the Willow Garden," like "Banks of the Ohio" and "Pretty Polly" is a beautiful melody with rather tragic lyrics. "Down in the Willow Garden" can be used for any number of beautiful mandolin solos with techniques ranging from the simplest single string picking, to single string solo with tremolo, to double stops, or like this solo, to crosspicking.

Crosspicking is a more advanced technique than most of the others we touched on in this book. This solo on "Down in the Willow Garden" is similar to the crosspicking solo on "Banks of the Ohio" (page 44). If you haven't already read through the introduction and worked on the "Banks of the Ohio" do that now. Briefly though, in crosspicking we'll set up a three note pattern: on strings 4-2-3 or 3-1-2. We'll generally play the melody note on the lowest and first string we play. The other two notes will be drone notes that flesh out the chord. There will be places in the solo (measures 2, 6, 10, 14, 18, 22, 26, 30) where we won't play a complete three string pattern. In those cases we'll rock back and forth between one melody note and one drone note on two neighboring strings.

Pick directions and fretting finger suggestions on the three string pattern are crucial. Play a down stroke on the first note and up strokes on the two following notes. Pick directions are shown in the music above the tablature line. Down strokes are indicated by the down arrows, up strokes by the up arrows.

The chord positions you need to hold to play the solo are all pretty easy. The F in measure 17 is a bit of a stretch but I'm sure you can get it if you practice. ***Key of C.***

Soundhole & shoulder detail Pomeroy PA 4 mandolin, 2008

Down in the Willow Garden *crosspicking solo*

Arrangement © 2012 by Dix Bruce

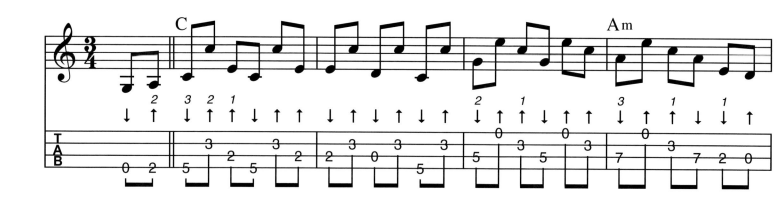

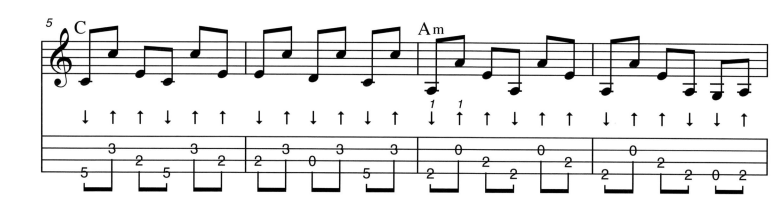

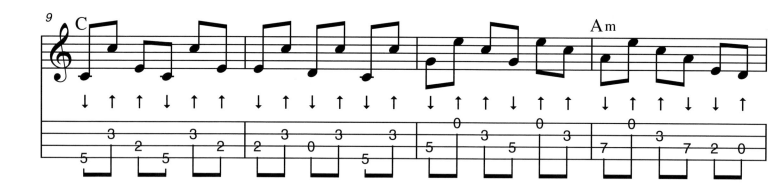

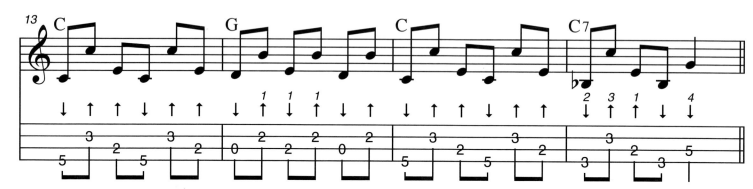

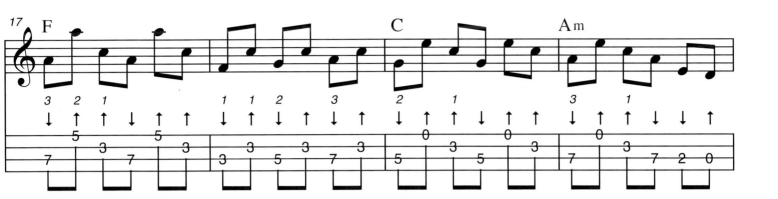

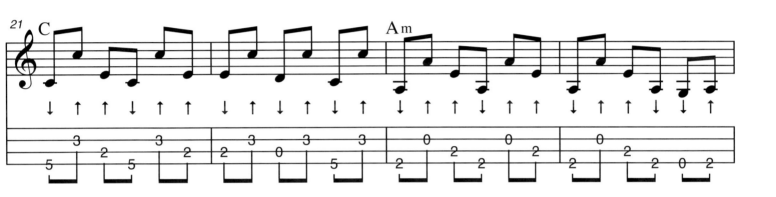

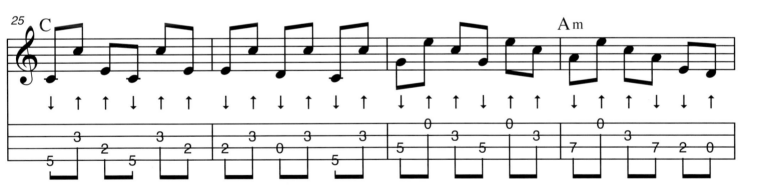

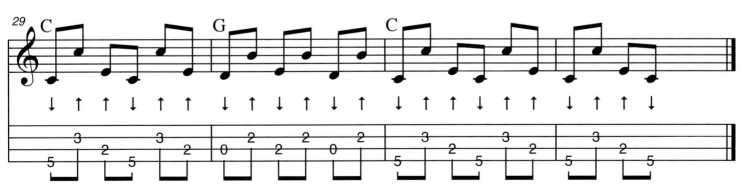

Index

Special thanks to Bob Bergman, Annette Slikker, Julie Cline,
Alison Stuart, and Chris McLaughlin for their most helpful suggestions.

This book is dedicated to the memory of my good friend Bob Schneider.
He was a musician, an engineer, and he built wonderful mandolins like the one above.